Living Your Best Life

with Help from Your

Guardian Angel

ROBBIE HOLZ

2

Day 1

Your guardian angel loves you unconditionally and can powerfully assist you in all aspects of life.

Who Are Angels and Guardian Angels?

Angels are etheric, androgynous, immortal beings of light. They assist human-kind with matters both small and large. They are willing and able to help you enhance your life. The angelic realm is here to serve and be called upon when needed. Whenever you engage their help, your life will change for the better.

Every single person on Earth has at least one guardian angel assigned to them You are *never* without the presence of an angelic being. A guardian angel is by your side from your first breath to your last.

A guardian angel's role is to protect you according to your soul's intentions. They ensure you're not harmed, killed or exposed to things your soul does not intend for you to experience. Your guardian angel has saved you from harm many times without you knowing it. You don't need to know your guardian angel's name. Call them whatever feels right to you.

Angels love you just as you are and without judgment. Their love for you is far beyond human comprehension. They will never lose patience with you. They don't have that kind of emotion.

Initially, in this workbook, we are going to engage with your guardian angel because they are the easiest to communicate with. Guardian angels are de-signed to be the easiest to approach, even more than your soul, spirit guides, angels and archangels. You have access to help from any of these entities on the other side of the veil (an invisible barrier between our physical world and the spirit world), but it's not necessary to look beyond your guardian angel.

Do you recall any instances when some unseen force seemed to prevent you from injury? Write it down, briefly.

Have you ever knowingly utilized the assistance of your guardian angel?

Next, we will delve into other sources available to you for help such as archangels, Ascended Masters and benevolent spirit guides including deceased loved ones.

> *"Everyone has a guardian angel, and some people have more than one! Our guardian angels are messengers from God, sent to guide us as we make our way through life."*
> —Kimberly Marooney, author, angel expert

Day 2

*Spirit guides, archangels, and Ascended Masters
are all part of a spiritual team available to you.*

Who Are Archangels and Ascended Masters?

Your guardian angel is supported by various angels, spirit guides, archangels, and Ascended Masters. Unlike your guardian angel, they are not assigned to you specifically but will step forward to assist when needed.

They each bring something unique to the table. For example, Archangel Michael is often called upon for protection, while Archangel Raphael aids with healing. Archangels are incredibly powerful and the highest-ranking angels.

Although angels may briefly take on a human form to assist, they do not need to incarnate as a human being. An Ascended Master, however, is someone who has incarnated on Earth and undergone a series of spiritual transformations. A few of the commonly known Ascended Masters are Kwan Yin, Sanat Kumara, Buddha, Mary (mother of Jesus), Maitreya, Mary Magdalene and Lord Lanto.

Who Are Spirit Guides?

Each of us has several spirit guides at one time or another. Spirit guides are not angels but someone who has had several past incarnations as a human. They choose to remain as a disembodied spirit to be of service as a guide and protector to incarnated humans.

It's important to note that we are working *only with benevolent beings and spirit guides of light and love.* Whether existing as an angel, Ascended Master, guardian angel, spirit guide, archangel or spirit animal, the immense unconditional love they feel for you is beyond human grasp. They will not harm you in any way. We will not be engaging with malevolent beings.

A deceased loved one or an ancestor may choose to occasionally love, guide and protect you from the other side of the veil. You will not be "bothering" them or keeping them from doing other things as they can engage in many things at the same time.

There are many others also always available to you, for instance, spirit animals and totem animals, but we'll focus on your guardian angel.

Have you ever felt the presence of a deceased loved one? An unseen loving presence?

Is there an Ascended Master with whom you feel a strong connection?

Next, we explore why these benevolent beings from the other side of the veil are assisting us.

> *There are specific angels and guides who have been assigned to you for this lifetime. Other guides and angels will assist you temporarily according to your needs.*

Day 3

Here Is Why Angels and Spirit Guides Help Us.

Angels and spirit guides are on Earth to serve by choice. They are now here in *unprecedented* numbers to help bring about a global awakening. We are shifting into a higher consciousness that will create a love-based existence of harmony and peace. Angels and spirit guides are committed to serving humanity in this transformational time of awakening.

Their mission is also to help humankind realize our Divine Nature. They want to assist us to reach our highest potential where we can fully express our Divine qualities.

Here's Who You *Really* Are.

Divine Source (God/Goddess, Creator) experiences Itself by existing as a river, bird, mountain, tree, human . . . Everything in existence—from the smallest insect to the infinite galaxy—is a different form of Divine Source. At its most elemental level, everyone and everything is composed of Divine Source. We are all connected at our core by the same seed of life. You are one with all of life.

You are a fractal of Divine Source. If you think of Divine Source as the ocean, you are not a drop of the ocean but the entire ocean in a drop. You are the exact same *quality* of Divine Source but a smaller *quantity*. You are Divine.

You exist because Divine Source has a deep desire to be—to create. At this very moment, Divine Source is exploring and expressing through you. You are Divine Source experiencing life as an incarnated soul in a human body. A soul is an etheric, eternal being. You are a soul in a body—not a body with a soul.

Divine Source *loves* to create. Ask yourself, what you have created lately. It could even be a vegetable garden or unique meal.

Where do you feel a closer connection to Divine Source? In nature? In a sacred space?

Next, you will gain insight into the bigger picture of why you are here on Planet Earth.

> *The angels and guides are not up above but all around you.*

8

Day 4

Your soul has specific intentions on how you are to evolve. Everything and everyone is part of the process to help facilitate that growth.

The Soul Is the Animating Force in the Body.

A soul is an etheric animating force that inhabits the body and acts through it. It is like the hand in a puppet. When the hand (soul) is removed, the puppet (body) collapses. When a person dies, the soul leaves the physical body but continues as an eternal spirit in a different dimension.

Your soul contains the wisdom of *many* lifetimes. It is your soul's quest to grow and evolve. That's why a soul desires to reincarnate over and over again. It uses one body after another for growth, expanding into higher consciousness and embodying more of your true Divine nature.

Your Soul Determines the Methods of Self-Evolution.

Your soul plays a tremendous role in designing your life. Your life's journey will reflect what your soul intends for you to master. For instance, in this lifetime if your soul wants you to achieve deeper levels of forgiveness, it will put a plan in place with various opportunities for you to forgive others.

We are each learning different soul lessons in a myriad of ways. Some souls choose to attain greater levels of acceptance, self-love, and compassion. The possibilities for growth are endless.

You are *exactly* the way you need to be according to your soul's intentions for what you are here to learn. If you needed to be different, you would be different. Your soul deliberately chose a body, your family and specific experiences necessary to facilitate growth and evolution. You carry all the acquired knowledge forward as a soul.

If your soul wants you to feel more self-love, it may choose a family that does not love you. They may even lead you to believe you are not good enough. Your soul's intentions are for you to overcome this distorted belief and realize who you are: a glorious Divine being worthy of unconditional love. As you grow in self-love, you'll find the love from within rather than outside of you.

Is there a recurring challenge that continually shows up throughout your life?

Are there certain family members who are particularly difficult? Why?

In the next lesson we uncover why Earth is the perfect paradise and learning laboratory.

> *There are no accidents. Everything that happens to you is here to help you grow and evolve.*

Day 5

*Earth is a school for souls. There are endless
classrooms with souls evolving at their own pace.*

Earth Is a Paradise and a School for Souls.

For a soul—an etheric spirit—to have a physical body is a tremendous bless-ing. Although it may not feel like it at times, it is also a gift to have a wide range of human emotions. Your body and emotions are your tools for this Earth school.

Souls love incarnating on Earth for reasons other than experiencing a physi-cal body and different emotions. Earth is a free-will planet, which means you choose how to respond to the learning experiences your soul sets up for you. As you encounter your soul's learning opportunities, you choose whether to react from your mind or heart. Will you choose judgment and anger? Or will you respond from your Divine nature, with acceptance and compassion?

While your soul may have enrolled you in a specific course of study, you move at your own pace and decide whether you will graduate or not. If you resist learning Forgiveness 101, for example, you may find yourself repeating the class until you finally graduate. It should be noted that the forgiveness opportunities will intensify until you pass, whether in this lifetime or another.

Souls Are at Different Stages of Development.

Earth offers extremes of darkness and light. At one end of the spectrum are younger souls who tend to be materialistic, self-serving, greedy, judgmental, and vain. At the other end are older souls who are usually compassionate, loving, and feel a deep desire to be of service to others. These extreme di-versities provide contrasts which enable us to see things more clearly, just as contrasts in a painting define things more readily.

The shadow and light are needed not just in this Earth learning lab but within

11

each of us as well. Embrace the shadow aspects in you as much as you do the light, for they are all necessary elements to achieving higher consciousness.

No soul is *better* than another. We are all equal as souls but are simply at different stages of growth and development. Older souls are more evolved and enlightened than younger souls, like university students vs. primary schoolchildren.

It is not uncommon for an older soul to choose to be born into a family of younger souls. The contrasts between the different family members provide endless opportunities for growth for both the older and younger souls.

Name five things you are grateful for about your body.

Are there certain emotions which you regularly suppress?

Next, we expand on how the angels and spirit guides help you learn your soul's intended lessons.

"Sometimes the most evolved souls take on the most difficult paths. More learning can occur when there are many obstacles than when there are few or none. A life with difficult relationships, filled with obstacles and losses, presents the most opportunity for the soul's growth. You may have chosen the most difficult life so that you could accelerate your physical (spiritual) *progress."*
—Brian Weiss, author, psychiatrist

Day 6

Your guardian angel will not intervene on their own to assist with your struggles. You must ask for their help before they interfere on this free-will Earth.

It Is Necessary to Ask for Help from Angels and Guides Before They Intervene.

Earth is a school where souls bravely incarnate because of the tremendous opportunities for growth and evolution. However, it was never your soul's intention for you to attend this tough school unassisted. There is always help available from the other side at any given moment. Remember, your guardian angel *never* leaves your side during your lifetime.

Your guardian angel will not intrude except to protect you from harm, being killed, or experiencing something your soul does not intend for you.

Since Earth is a free-will planet, you make your own decisions. There are no "mistakes." There are certainly healthier and wiser choices, but your guardian angel knows you learn from everything, especially pain. There is nothing wrong with pain. It's one of the best catalysts for change.

Take the example of a wise, loving parent who watches as their child learns to tie his or her shoelaces. Even if the child gets the laces tangled up in knots, the parent knows it's all part of the learning process. If the child asks for help, then the parent assists in the best supportive way.

Your guardian angel understands choices that lead to painful consequences are often your greatest teachers. Adversity and difficult challenges lead to growth (which is why older souls sign up for them). Angels and spirit guides do not judge you or try to interfere with your learning process. They wait for you to ask for help.

Angels and guides will not infringe on your free will, even if your choices are leading you down a path of suffering. However, many of us are creating more pain and struggle than our souls intend.

They Respond to Your Requests According to Your Soul's Intentions.

Angels and guides are happy to step in when you ask for their help. When you do ask, they *always* respond. Every. Single. Time. They respond according to your soul's intentions, and the highest good of all. That last sentence is crucial and worth repeating: They respond according to your soul's intentions, and the highest good of all.

For instance, you can ask them to help you win the lottery to ease your financial burdens during the pandemic, but if it is not your soul's intentions to do so (which it likely is not), they won't assist you in hitting the $40-million Jackpot. However, they will follow your soul's desires and bring you money in other ways.

Your guardian angel is here to help you accomplish your soul's desires. While your guardian angel is the first in line to assist you, *everyone* from the other side of the veil is available to you as well.

The intention is that you have powerful assistance always accessible. You are not going through this journey alone. You are supposed to be using their help.

You might feel better knowing that every time you allow them to help you, they grow and evolve because they are serving you out of tremendous love. It is a symbiotic relationship between you, the angels and the guides.

Do you recall a circumstance when the angels or guides assisted you after you asked for their help? Why don't you ask for their help more often?

Next, I will explain how Spiritual and Universal Laws control how the angels and guides respond to your requests.

> *Angels are in your life to be of service, but you must*
> *invite them to take part. They respect your free will*
> *too much to simply intrude into your world uninvited.*

Day 7

*Angels and guides respond to each request according to
the highest good of all and all of your soul's intentions.*

Angels and Guides Are Governed by Spiritual Laws.

All angels and spirit guides are governed by Spiritual Laws. One specific Spiritual Law is to not interfere with free will. Based on that Spiritual Law, if you ask your angels and guides to help your brother-in-law find a job during the pandemic, they will not intervene unless *he* asks for their help. Earth is a free-will planet and the angels and guides will never force anyone to do anything against their will.

The angels and guides know pain and struggle are part of the learning process. They also see the bigger picture and understand the soul's intentions. For instance, your brother-in-law's soul may want him to become less materialistic.

The angels and guides must always follow the soul's desires. They are not allowed to assist in opposition to the soul's intentions. However, the angels and guides are always allowed to send love. At your request to help your brother-in-law, they will send him the energy of love. It is up to your brother-in-law whether he accepts or rejects that love.

One of the biggest limitations for angels and guides is the restriction that requires them to respond to you per your soul's intentions. If your soul desires you to achieve mastery over self-forgiveness, you may have been deliberately born into an obese family who conditioned you during childhood with unhealthy eating habits.

You may be extremely overweight and berate yourself for not conforming to society's standards of beauty. Your soul may want you to experience being overweight to help you learn to love yourself *exactly* as you are. You may ask your angels to help you lose excess weight because you hate how you look.

Your angels understand the extra weight is a method to help you learn to love yourself. The angels will help you learn to love yourself first before they then help you lose weight. They cannot eliminate the excess weight while it is still needed as a tool to help you overcome self-criticism.

Universal Laws Limit How Angels and Guides Respond.

Angels and spirit guides are also limited by Universal Laws. One Universal Law prohibits the angels and guides from healing someone's body when it is physically no longer capable of healing itself. Say you ask the angels to help you heal from Stage IV breast cancer, for example; they will not do so if your body is incapable of healing at that advanced stage of the disease. However, they will assist you in coping with the cancer. They may send you pain relief, acceptance, and peace. Despite your pleas, they will not interfere if your soul is using that illness as a method for you to physically pass and return home.

Angels and guides also will not completely heal something if it's still needed for soul growth. For instance, if you became severely ill from a illness because your soul wanted you to develop deeper compassion, your angels would have permission to heal you only *after* you acquired compassion for others.

Once you have requested help from the angels and guides, release all expectations about their response. They are aware of every single plea and are fulfilling each request according to your soul's intentions, the highest good of all, and the governing Spiritual and Universal Laws.

Have you requested help from the angels but they did not respond in the way you expected?

Next, you will learn how to specifically ask for angelic assistance.

---

*Release expectations of how the angels and
guides will respond to your request for help.*

Day 8

You Ask for Help Through Your Thoughts.

Asking for help from the angels and spirit guides is incredibly easy. You simply ask in your mind. They are telepathic to your thoughts. Asking once in your mind is all you need to do.

They respond to every request (according to your soul's intentions and desires). That is why we don't say *"Please help me,"* but rather, in advance, say *"Thank you for helping me."*

Ask as often as you like and for whatever you need. It does not matter whether it is big, small, vague, or specific. The possibilities are limitless.

For example, you can ask for any or all of the following:

- "Thank you for bringing abundance into my life."
- "Thank you for helping me develop healthier eating habits."
- "Thank you for helping me be the best daughter/son, mother/father, partner, grandmother/grandfather I can be."
- "Thank you for helping me create a healthy and vibrant body."
- "Thank you for helping me let go of what is in my best interests to release."
- "Thank you for helping me open up to what is in my best interests."
- "Thank you for helping me find a fulfilling career."
- "Thank you for helping me live the highest vision of my soul."

Although your guardian angel is the first to assist you, others may step forward at the request of your guardian angel. You don't need to know specifically who is helping you. Just send your gratitude.

What are some things you would like your angels and guides to help you with?

Next, you will discover some of the specific ways the angels and spirit guides can help you.

Ask for their help as often as you like.

Day 9

When you enlist the assistance of your angels and guides, you can shift from 5 amps of power to 5,000 amps of power in an instant.

There Are Endless Ways Angels and Guides Can Help You.

Your guardian angels and spirit guides have many ways to assist you. The intent was always that you utilize their tremendous help. You do not live your life unassisted.

Helping you is as easy as child's play for them. The challenge is getting your resistant mind to go in the direction they are trying to guide you. They always honor your free will, so they will never force you to do anything.

Here are a few of the many ways they can help *once you've asked for their assistance:*

They download energies into you. If you have difficulty forgiving someone, they will continually send you the energy of forgiveness.

They provide clarity. If you struggle to understand why the same difficult events keep occurring, they can help you understand the message behind these challenges.

They provide protection. If you are traveling by plane or driving in unfamiliar areas, they can help you arrive safely to your destination.

They soften triggers and help you unhook more easily. When you get caught up in negativity—criticism, judgment, anxiety—the angels and guides can help you shift to love-based thoughts and emotions. You emerge from the dark alleys of negativity more quickly and eventually stop entering them.

They help you find awe in everyday moments. When asked, the angels can help you feel the wonder and joy in your everyday life.

They help you eliminate stress and fear. The angels and guides can help you find relief from anxiety and worry. With their assistance you can live a happier, more confident and peaceful life.

It may be easier to ask for help if you remember that every time you allow the angels and guides to assist you, they evolve because they are serving out of tremendous love. It's a win/win for everyone, so ask away.

What frustrating issues can they help you resolve?

What positive energies do you need more of? Patience? Acceptance? Self-love?

Tomorrow we expand on more ways the angels and guides can help you.

The angels and guides will **never** *force you to do anything.*

Day 10

Angels and Guides Can Assist You with Everything from the Everyday to a Crisis.

When you utilize the unlimited capabilities of angels and guides, you are vastly empowering your life. They can help you in any area of your life. Here are more ways they can assist you.

They increase your consciousness. Like pieces of a puzzle that eventually fit together, angels and guides feed you aha moments. Comments from strangers, scenarios played out before you, and recommended books help you gain insights that raise your consciousness.

They easily create synchronicities. It is effortless for the angels and guides to create synchronicities. Again, it's child's play for them. Synchronicities are one of the ways they bring insight and create alignment.

Flow happens with angelic involvement. When you follow your soul's desires, it feels right, fulfilling, and things fall into place. Angels and guides can help you discover your soul's intended path, whether it's a career, a romantic partner or a humanitarian purpose.

They help you lead a balanced, healthier life. Angels and guides can help you release unhealthy mindsets and distortions. They can help you release guilt about weight gain. They can motivate you to exercise daily and eat healthier. They can help you nurture yourself.

They assist you with the little things. Angels know it is the simple, everyday things that go wrong and collectively cause stress. They can assist with the mundane aspects of life to keep everything running more smoothly.

They help you discover the best direction. No matter what you struggle

21

with, angels and guides can assist you in choosing the best path to reach your goals.

What have you been struggling with that angels and guides can assist you with?

Next, we explore your mind's role as a powerful tool and its limitations.

> *The angels and guides can show you the easier and better way. They do not have the limitations we do.*

Day 11

Your mind is a powerful tool. However, it was never supposed to be in control of your life. Your mind doesn't know the best way to recover from an illness, but a higher consciousness does. Hand over your issues to a higher consciousness and let it, not your mind, steer you through challenges.

Your Mind Is a Servant to Your Soul.

Your mind is an incredibly powerful tool. It is important to remember, though, that it is just that—a tool. Your mind is intended to be a servant to your soul. Your soul is supposed to be in charge, not your mind. Most of us are utilizing the mind in ways never intended.

Your mind doesn't know the best way to find the right long-term romantic partner or how to achieve a fulfilling career. Your mind does not know how to be an excellent parent or partner. These are things that a higher consciousness—Divine Source, your soul, angels, guides—does know.

A higher consciousness knows what your soul intends to achieve in this lifetime, and how best to achieve it. A higher consciousness knows the best career and partner(s) for this life's journey. The mind is designed to intuitively follow guidance from a higher consciousness on these matters.

Although your mind wants to control everything, it is intended to serve your soul, not be in charge. We get into trouble by using our minds to make decisions it is not equipped to make, such as where to live, how to make money, how to find like-minded friends, or how to heal.

The world reflects what happens when our minds are in control. The results are rampant negativity, fear, materiality, greed, genocide, war, etc.

Allow a Higher Consciousness to Help You Achieve Your Goals.

The best way to achieve any goal is to hand it over to a higher consciousness. Your mind is designed to intuitively receive and follow guidance from a higher consciousness: your soul, Higher Self, Oversoul, angel, benevolent spirit guide, Divine Source, God/Goddess. Remove your mind from behind the "steering wheel" and put a higher consciousness there instead. The mind is too fearful, limited and egoic to be in the driver's seat.

Allow this higher consciousness to guide and help you. Shift your mind into its intended role of "support staff" for your soul. Keep your mind excited and curious but not grabbing the wheel to control the journey.

Whenever you engage the services of your angels and guides, your mind needs to let go of two burning questions: "How?" and "When?" The mind tends to be a control freak and wants everything mapped out.

Like an anxious child, it is perpetually asking: "How are we going to get there? Are we there yet?" You've got to release the desire to control. Allow this higher consciousness to show you the better, easier, more fulfilling way. When your mind shifts into its intended supportive role, it eventually stops stressing about what to do. Relax. You are in incredibly capable and loving hands.

What have you been trying to figure out that you can hand over to your angels and guides?

Next, you will learn the different ways angels and guides communicate with you.

> *Our chaotic world demonstrates what*
> *happens when our minds are in control.*

Day 12

You Have the Ability to Recognize Communication from Angels and Guides.

Angels and guides communicate with you through different methods. You recognize their communication based on the way you were programmed in each lifetime. Everyone is clairsentient, meaning they feel or sense guidance within their body, especially in the chest area. They have a strong feeling or a "knowing" about something.

Very few people are clairvoyant, where they "see" images in their mind, including future events. Also uncommon are people with the capability of clairaudience, where they "hear" what is inaudible.

Another uncommon ability is clairscent, where you psychically "smell" without using your nose. For example, when thinking of your deceased grandfather, you may smell (not imagine) the scent of his pipe. Also rare is someone who has the capability of clairgustance, which means they "taste" something without putting anything in their mouth.

Everyone is born clairsentient, but very few people have the other "clair" abilities. We are designed to use our clairsentient capability to guide us throughout our lives. We will explore in the coming weeks how to tap into your clairsentience and significantly develop that ability.

It's easier to recognize signs from angels and guides if you release any preconceived beliefs about how and when their messages manifest. They will respond in the way and time that's best.

Although your ability to identify their messages may be a bit rusty, the skill improves with practice. While it is highly unlikely that you will ever see or hear your guides and angels, you will sense their guidance.

Can you recall instances where you had a strong knowing about something?

Next, you will learn some of the ways angels and guides send you messages and guidance.

> *It is highly unlikely you will see or hear your angels and guides in this lifetime, but with practice you will feel them.*

Day 13

Your ability to perceive signs from your angels will become sharper.

Your Ability to Notice Signs Will Improve with Increased Awareness.

After you have asked for help from your angels and guides, you will begin to recognize their messages and signs all around you. Here are a few of the methods angels, guides and deceased loved ones use to guide and help you.

Recurring Thoughts – When the same thoughts continue to pop into your mind out of nowhere, pay attention.

Intuition – Your sixth sense, or intuition, is your primary inner compass and the main method angels and guides connect with you.

Automatic Writing – Write in longhand or type on a computer as fast as you can. Do not try to consciously control what you write. This is an effective way to receive a stream of consciousness type of guidance from angels and guides.

Dreams – Dreams are a common method of contact from deceased loved ones, angels and guides.

Ringing in Your Ears, Goosebumps or Chills – When not caused by a medical condition, ringing in your ears, goosebumps, chills or tingling in your body are ways angels and guides convey their presence.

Meditation – When you quiet your busy mind, it is much easier to sense the subtle messages from your angels and guides.

Muscle Testing or Dowsing – Ask a question and use muscle testing, dowsing or a pendulum to get directions from your angels and guides. Be careful that your mind is not attached to a specific answer and influencing the results.

Instantaneous Answer to a Question – An immediate response in your mind to a question you just asked angels or guides is usually from them. The second or third responses are often created by your mind.

Song Lyrics – Song lyrics spontaneously playing in your mind often convey guidance.

Aha Moments – Sudden insights are usually from angels or guides.

Have you experienced any of the above?

There are additional ways in which you are guided and helped by angels and guides. We explore those methods next.

> *"Signs are everywhere. We just need to recognize them."*
> —Melanie Barnum, psychic medium, author

Day 14

You are designed to recognize guidance from the celestial realms, especially from your guardian angel. Trust in your ability to intuitively sense their guidance.

There Are Many Different Methods Used to Communicate with You.

It is easy for angels and guides to communicate with you. You are designed to recognize their guidance and understand their messages. Trust that. Here are additional methods angels and guides use to guide and assist you.

Electricity – Manipulating electricity is a very common method of communication, especially from deceased loved ones. The computer may glitch or shut off, a television may spontaneously turn on and off, radio volume may suddenly rise, the phone rings with no one on the other end, lights dim or turn on.

First Thought Upon Awakening – When you awaken during the night or in the morning, your first thought is often a message from angels and guides. The second or third thought is usually from your mind.

You Sneeze, Trip or Drop Something – When you are startled by a loud noise, trip or sneeze, pay attention to what you were just thinking or doing. Angels and guides sometimes use these disruptions to get your attention and help you become more mindful. They are likely encouraging you to redirect your thoughts or actions to be of a healthier and more supportive nature.

Numbers – Recurring numbers or numbers on a clock when you suddenly awaken often relay messages. See *Angel Numbers* and *Angel Numbers: 101* by Doreen Virtue for their specific meaning.

Recurring Suggestions – If you receive the same suggestion from different sources, it is often guidance from your guides and angels. For example, the second or third time a particular job is suggested by a different source, angels may be guiding you to apply for a specific job.

Telepathy – Angels and guides communicate by sending thoughts directly to your mind.

Symbols – Another means of communication is symbolism. Random findings of specific objects such as coins or feathers may signify angelic presence.

Nature – Deceased loved ones will often make their presence known through objects that have a significant connection to them such as butterflies, lady-bugs or specific flowers. Angels and guides also use recurring animals and birds to convey messages. For their meaning, refer to *Animal Speak* and *Nature-Speak* by Ted Andrews.

Coincidence, Synchronicity – Serendipity, synchronicity or coincidence are a validation of assistance from angels and guides.

Gut Instinct – Your gut instinct is a communication tool to guide you, especially in making decisions. You know in three seconds whether something feels right or not. If it takes longer than three seconds, your mind is now engaged.

Your guardian angel is the easiest spirit being for you to communicate with. Commune primarily with your guardian angel in the beginning stages. If you do not understand the message angels and guides sent you, ask your guardian angel to clarify it for you. When have you experienced any of the above?

Next, you will discover how to differentiate guidance coming from your mind and that coming from angels and guides.

"Electricity is a very popular way in which spirits send us signs, because of the energy connection . . . When we cross over, we are in pure energy form, and we have the ability to blend with the electrical currents and manipulate the flow. This is why we see lights dim or switch off, see televisions turn on or off for no apparent reason, and hear phones ring with no physical caller on the other end."
—Bill Philipps, author, psychic medium

Day 15

Don't Worry About Your Ability to Communicate with Each Other.

Angels and guides are excellent at conveying their guidance to you. If you need to know something, they will find a way to get their message across. They will use different methods of communicating their guidance. The second or third time you get the same message, you should pay attention. Angels and guides do whatever it takes to get their message across to you. If you are not getting any messages, it's likely there aren't any at that moment.

You Can Distinguish Messages from Your Mind vs. Angels and Guides.

A common concern is how to differentiate whether messages are coming from your mind or from angels and guides. Your mind will insist that you have to, should or need to do something. Your mind is fear-based and sometimes operates out of guilt.

Guidance from your angels and guides is based in love. They will lovingly guide you with your intuition, sixth sense and gut instinct. Their guidance *feels* right. Angels and guides will never insist or force you to do anything. The mind is guiding you from fear, while angels and guides are guiding you from love. If you are still uncertain, ask yourself: *What would love do in this situation?*

Do not be concerned about their ability to convey their messages to you, and your ability to recognize their guidance and understand it. Everyone is designed to communicate together. If you miss their signs, they will continue to use different means to get their message across until you finally get it.

If you misinterpret their guidance, they will use different ways to clarify their message. They will persist until you get it. Relax and trust in this process. Over time you will become more adept at recognizing and interpreting their messages.

Have you encountered instances when you knew something but could not explain how you knew it?

Next, you will learn how to strengthen your intuition—the main method of communication with your angels and guides.

Your mind guides you with fear. The guides and angels guide you with love.

Day 16

> *Guidance from the angels and guides will come*
> *from your intuition. Tune into your intuition often.*

Intuition Is How the Subconscious Communicates to Your Conscious Mind.

Intuition is one of the most powerful tools available to you. Sometimes referred to as your sixth sense, gut instinct, or inner GPS, your intuition is the ability to understand something without the need for analytical reasoning. It is how angels, spirit guides and your soul communicate with your conscious mind. That's why it is such an effective source of inner wisdom and guidance.

Everyone has intuition but it's developed in us to varying degrees. Like a muscle, the more you use your intuition the stronger it grows.

Intuition may be felt in several ways. You experience a sudden hunch or insight. You feel a physical sensation throughout your body. You feel uneasiness or suspicion toward something or someone.

Here are a few methods to strengthen your intuition.

Meditate. The most effective way to develop your intuition is to meditate. You must quiet your chatty mind to feel the subtle guidance from angels and guides. When your mind is still, you feel your intuition over your fears. Develop a meditation practice of quieting your mind a minimum of ten minutes a day.

Create Solitary Moments. If possible, find ways to take a few minutes to separate yourself from others. Turn your attention inward and just *feel*, don't *think*. Your intuition feels. Your mind thinks—incessantly. Try to intuitively sense the answer to a question. Differentiate whether you are *feeling* or *thinking* responses.

Listen to Your Body. Your body is a conduit for your intuition. That's why it's extremely important to pay attention to your gut feelings. Your mind will lie to you, but your body never will.

Research How to Develop Your Intuition. There are several books on how to boost your intuition. A couple of good ones are *Developing Intuition* by Shakti Gawain and *Trust Your Vibes* by Sonia Choquette.

Your intuition is a valuable, effective tool. It will not steer you wrong. You are accessing powerful inner wisdom designed to help you navigate life easier. The stronger your intuition, the easier it is to communicate with your angels and guides.

How often do you tune into your intuition throughout the day?

Next, we explore the tremendous benefits of meditation.

"Intuition is the whisper of the soul."
—Jiddy Krishnamurti, philosopher, speaker, writer

Day 17

The Benefits of Meditating Are Extensive.

Incessant thinking is rampant in our world and incredibly unhealthy. It is imperative to free yourself of involuntary internal dialogue. That is why meditation is one of the most powerful and effective things you can do.

Quieting your mind in meditation for only five minutes is beneficial. Meditation is one of the best ways to loosen the grip of sticky emotions. You can feel the inner sanctum of peace when you switch off the incessant mind chatter.

The health advantages of meditation are impressive. Thousands of scientific studies have shown the benefits include stress reduction, better sleep, lower blood pressure, decreased depression and anxiety, improved cardiovascular function and strengthened immunity. Meditation reduces physical pain, accelerates healing, and promotes wellness of body, mind, and spirit. And it doesn't end there.

Meditating only 5-10 minutes a day instantly calms your mind and lifts your mood. You will feel increased peace, clarity, and confidence. Through meditating, you stop unhealthy thought patterns and, using visualizations, create the life you desire.

Importantly, meditation expands your intuition, develops greater consciousness and enlightenment. Mediating can build a stronger connection to angels and spirit guides. When you silence your busy mind in meditation, you can feel the subtle inner guidance of your soul, angels, and guides.

Developing a daily meditation practice is one of the most important things you can do to improve the quality of our life. Silencing your mind for ten minutes a day will vastly enrich your well-being. If you believe you do not have ten minutes a day to quiet your mind, you *really* do need to meditate.

Start a meditation practice by committing to a minimum of five minutes a day to quiet your mind and focus on your breath.

Next, you will learn about the different types of meditations.

"Messages flow better when the mind is quiet and calm."
—Toni Klein, author

Day 18

Meditation Is Essential to Living a Healthy Life.

You already know the long list of impressive benefits that will come with meditation. What you may not know is how to develop a regular meditation practice. No doubt you have a busy life and a busy mind. Meditation is extremely simple and very doable, no matter what is happening in your life.

There are two types of meditations: active and passive. Active meditation is when your body is engaged in a repetitive activity and your mind is focused exclusively on that activity. A few examples of an active meditation are washing the dishes or the car, running, cooking, gardening, knitting, painting or mowing the lawn. Your mind and all your senses are completely focused on the task at hand and not wandering off into idle thoughts.

Passive meditation is the act of quieting your mind while remaining physically still. In a passive meditation you focus on your breathing, the flame of a candle, or silently repeat a mantra like "OM" on the in-breath and "MA" on the out-breath.

You make *anything* a meditation by completely focusing on it and engaging your senses. Smell the different garden or kitchen scents. Feel the lawn mower vibrating throughout your hands and arms. Listen to the tree leaves rustle or the hum of the appliances. Watch the clouds roll gently across the sky or a bee flit from flower to flower.

The principle of meditating is simple. You practice controlling your mind, rather than your mind controlling you. You are training your mind to focus rather than wander, so you are no longer a slave to your incessant thinking. You learn to consciously think supportive thoughts rather than sabotaging ones. Meditation helps you gain mastery over your thoughts and that is why it is such a powerful thing.

Avoid judging whether your meditation was successful. Thoughts will materialize. Do not get frustrated. It's the nature of the mind. When thoughts emerge—and they will—gently bring your focus back to your meditation.

Try a passive meditation for five minutes. Try an active meditation for five minutes.

A simple and easy meditation will be outlined in the next lesson with more in the back of the book.

> *"A quiet mind is able to hear intuition over fear."*
> —Yvan Byeajee, author

Day 19

It's Vital to Quiet Your Mind Every Day.

Meditating is quieting your busy chatty mind. Commit to meditating 5-10 minutes each day. It's better to meditate 5-10 minutes a day than a continuous 60 minutes once a week. The goal is to develop a *daily* habit of giving yourself a break from your mind chatter. If you can't meditate one day for the committed time, then get quiet for just a few minutes. Don't complicate meditation.

Here's an easy game plan to meditate daily:

Get comfortable in a place where you will not be disturbed when you meditate. Find a quiet spot on a park bench, a cushion or pillow on the floor, a couch in a dimly lit room.

Use a timer so you don't have to keep an eye on the clock or worry about falling asleep. A popular free one is "Insight Timer" which is available for iPhone and Android. "Meditate for iPhone" will give you stats on your meditation practice.

Commit to meditating five minutes a day. Start small to avoid failing. To form a long-lasting habit, you need to be consistent, so start with something very easy. On one day if you feel like meditating for ten minutes, go for it, but you're *committed* to only five minutes each day.

Once you've meditated five minutes for seven days straight, then meditate for seven minutes each day. If you stick to that for 21 days straight, then add 1-3 minutes to your practice until you build up to 30 minutes a day.

Sitting with your eyes and mouth closed, **focus on your breath**. Follow your breath as it enters your nose and moves to your throat, then inflates your lungs and belly. Continue to *effortlessly* follow your breath as it moves out of your deflating lungs, into your throat and out your nose. If it's helpful, you can inhale for the count of five seconds, hold your breath for five seconds and exhale for five seconds. Observe your breath without overanalyzing or thinking about it.

It's not a matter of *if* your mind will wander but *when*. When it does, **gently bring the focus back to your breathing**. If your thoughts wander into how bored you are, bring your attention back to your breathing. If your to-do list pops into your mind, patiently bring your focus back to your breathing. Focus on your breath; the mind wanders, bring your thoughts back to your breath; the mind wanders, bring your thoughts back to your breath . . .

You're training your mind to focus, concentrate and let go, and not wander off. Like learning any new skill, it may be awkward at first, but you'll get better at it the more you do it. **Be kind and extra patient with yourself** as you gradually get the hang of it.

After your timer sounds, **finish your meditation by "grounding,"** i.e. imagine your feet growing roots to the center of the earth.

Do not feel like you failed—no matter how much your mind wandered. If you managed to quiet your mind for just a few minutes combined, it was a successful meditation.

Try the above meditation at least once this week. There are additional meditations at the end of the book.

The next lesson offers a meditation to connect to angels and spirit guides.

> *"The answers you seek never come when the*
> *mind is busy. They come when the mind is still."*
> —Author Unknown

Day 20

> *Communicating with your guides and angels*
> *will produce greater insight and peace.*

Meditation to Connect to Angels and Guides

It's a good idea to develop a practice of meditating in the same location around the same time each day.

- Get into a comfortable seated position. Close your eyes and take three deep breaths, inhaling and exhaling slowly, relaxing a little more with each breath.

- In your mind, create a safe environment. Envision an inviting place where you will always meet with your angels or guides. You could be strolling through a garden gate, down a flower-lined path, across a meadow or sitting on a bench next to a waterfall. You might see yourself seated in a rocking chair next to a crackling fireplace with an empty chair across from you where your angel will join you. If you prefer the seaside, you may imagine yourself walking along a deserted beach as warm foamy waves wash over your bare feet.

- When your mind is in a serene environment, get comfortable either sitting still or walking slowly, then call to your angels or guides and invite them to join you. Imagine they are next to you, hearing your every thought. Ask questions if you like. It's unlikely you will get a response in that moment. In the days and weeks that follow, you will probably receive subtle answers to some of those questions.

- When you have finished a dialogue with your angels or guides, thank them for joining you. Walk back down the path you came, closing the gate behind you. Imagine tree roots sprouting from the soles of your feet and growing to the center of the Earth. After 15 seconds, bring your focus back to your breath. Take three deep, slow breaths and gradually open your eyes.

Even if you didn't sense anything, your angels and guides were by your side and completely aware of your thoughts.

Try the above meditation at least once.

Next, we will discuss ways to develop a closer relationship with your angels and guides.

It is easier to connect during meditation
when your mind is calm, quiet and receptive.

Day 21

Developing a Closer Connection to Angels and Guides Will Profoundly Impact Your Life.

A relationship with your angels and guides is similar to that of a good friend: it requires nurturing. It's hard to develop a closer connection to them if you don't reach out regularly. Spend quality time with your angels and guides just as you would with a cherished friend.

You can't do this just once every few weeks but often. Consistency is key.

Here are a few ways to develop a stronger relationship with your angels and guides.

- Ask them to help you be more conscious, throughout your day, of them lovingly walking by your side.

- Request they be with you in a more mindful way, and then pay attention to the energy developing around and within you. You may feel a warm, loving presence. Keep in mind that not everyone feels energy.

- Develop stronger intuition. Angels and guides communicate with you through your intuition, which may be a bit weak and out of practice. Use the suggestions for Day 16 to increase your intuitive muscle.

- Record in a journal whenever you experience synchronicities, validations of their presence or assistance. Don't just put your journal in a drawer and forget about it, though. Refer to it often.

- Create a sacred space in a dedicated place in your home or yard. Over time, this sacred space will become filled with higher-vibrational energy that will make it easier to connect to your angels and guides.

- Add a shrine to your sacred space which may include pictures or statues of angels, spirit guides, ancestors, or deceased loved ones. Include white unscented candles, incense, and crystals. It's a lovely gesture to add fresh flowers, preferably white roses, which have the highest frequency of all flowers.

- It is important to meditate in your sacred space daily to steadily build the energy there. As previously mentioned, it is better to meditate a minimum of 5-10 minutes a day, rather than an hour once a week.

Release any expectations of how or when your relationship with your angels and guides will grow into a stronger bond. Be patient. If you ask angels and guides to develop a stronger connection and you follow the suggestions outlined above, it will happen.

Ask your angels and guides to help you develop a closer connection with them.

Next, you will discover the distinction between your soul and your Higher Self.

"I personally define spirit guides as a team of energetic beings that you have carefully chosen before your present incarnation. In turn, your spirit team has mutually agreed to guide you. These spirit guides reside in various levels and dimensions of the Spirit realms and usually communicate through thought and feeling."
—James Van Praagh, author, clairvoyant, medium

Day 22

*Adversities are deliberately in your life as
opportunities for your soul to master challenges.*

Your Higher Self Is a Smaller Aspect of Your Soul.

Your soul is different than your Higher Self. Your Higher Self is a small portion of your soul which is contained in your body. Your body could not possibly handle your entire soul. It's too much. Your Higher Self has a higher consciousness and helps you navigate this challenging dimension with a physical body and a wider range of emotions. Integrating your Higher Self's wisdom is an important aspect of your spiritual growth and evolution.

Your soul plays a tremendous role in deciding what you will learn in each lifetime. Your soul chooses a body that is perfect for what you are here to master. Just as Earth offers darkness and light, your soul has designed you to have both shadow and light. Embrace the shadow in you as much as you do the light. The shadow is necessary to help you see things more clearly.

You Grow Faster through Adversity.

Each of us is a soul learning at our own unique pace. We are all equal as souls; we are simply at different stages of evolution. Older souls are more advanced in their growth. An older, more developed soul will take on a more challenging curriculum at this Earth school. You wouldn't enroll in first-grade classes when you are well beyond high school.

If you are an advanced soul, you may sign up to get your Ph.D. or doctorate at this Earth school because you are equipped to handle a more difficult curriculum. You also have limitless help available from the other side of the veil.

There Are No Mistakes in Earth School.

While you are attending this Earth school, remember that there are no "mistakes." There are healthier and better choices but there are no mistakes because *everything* is a learning experience. Choices that create our most painful experiences are usually our best teachers. *There is nothing wrong with pain.*

There. Is. Nothing. Wrong. With. Pain.

Pain is a powerful teacher and catalyst for change. Allow any emotional and physical pain to tell you what needs to be addressed.

When you are in pain, ask yourself: *Why is this on my path? What am I resisting and why? How is this challenge here to help me grow as a soul?*

Focus inward for guidance from your Higher Self, angels and guides. Ask for their help in mastering this difficulty. Utilize their assistance to "pass" this lesson with flying colors, so you obtain your Ph.D. and move on.

Next, we discuss the roles other souls have agreed to play in your life.

"Souls take on this dense, uncomfortable world of matter to develop their awareness by living various experiences (such as fear, loneliness, and isolation) that are not available to them in other realms. But we are never alone. We have our guides."
—James Van Praagh, author, clairvoyant, medium

Day 23

> *Certain family members are often catalysts for your growth.*

Many in Your Life Agreed to Play Different Roles for Your Soul's Growth.

You incarnated on Earth primarily for soul growth. Each person is on a unique journey deliberately designed for what their soul wants them to explore and eventually master. You have "soul contracts" with other souls who agreed to play specific roles in this lifetime to help you accomplish this growth.

There are very thoughtful reasons behind who is in your life, especially your family members. It's not uncommon for an older soul to incarnate into a family of younger souls. That may explain why you don't fit in or you're the "black sheep." You each have much to teach one another, regardless of where you are on the soul-growth spectrum.

Everyone Is Deliberately in Your Path to Help You Evolve, Especially Family.

The most challenging people in your life are your greatest blessings. They have the most to teach you. They are playing a specific role with award-worthy performances as a catalyst for you. Since you can't always get away from family, they are phenomenal at teaching important lessons.

For instance, many older souls choose to master self-love—the need to find love from *within* no matter what everyone is telling you. Significant family members will withhold love. They lead you to believe you aren't pretty enough, smart enough, athletic enough, _____ enough. According to your soul's intentions, they are excellent in conditioning you to believe you are these "not enough" things.

Your soul intends you to *now* recognize who you *really* are: a Divine luminous being, a fractal of Divine Source, a glorious being of sound and light designed exactly the way you need to be for this journey. Can you overcome misperceptions about yourself and learn to deeply love *all* parts of you? You're capable of tremendous self-love. Don't let your mind talk you out of it.

If you are here to achieve deeper levels of forgiveness, your family may be providing you many advanced-soul opportunities to forgive them. Appreciate the most challenging people because the bigger the challenge, the greater the growth potential. Feel gratitude for what they are helping you gain mastery over. In their assigned role, they are helping you achieve in one lifetime what may normally take several.

You'll find inner peace when your mind stops resisting the family your soul has deliberately chosen for you. Don't forget: You were involved in the selection process. Recognize the gift in the challenges your family presents to you.

Who are the most challenging people in your life?

What are they here to help you master: Acceptance? Forgiveness? Self-love?

Next, we explore why recurring events happen to you.

"Every event we experience and every person we meet has intentionally been put in our path to help raise our level of consciousness."
—Cheryl Richardson, best-selling author

Day 24

It is paramount to accept others rather than judge them.

Everyone Is at Different Stages of Soul Growth.

Each person is on a unique journey designed for what their soul wants them to experience and master. We have soul contracts with other souls to play various roles to help us gain that mastery. For example, your soul may choose to develop higher levels of acceptance.

You will encounter all kinds of opportunities to move beyond your mind's criticism and judgment, and shift into acceptance and compassion. Can you accept and love everyone exactly the way they are, especially those in earlier stages of soul growth? Keep in mind, *no one* is broken and needs to be fixed.

No one is any better or less than another because of where they are in their soul's evolution and the lessons they are learning. Everyone is doing the best they can with where they are at their stage of development. We're each growing at our own pace and what we are presently capable of.

No matter where anyone is on their evolutionary path (including yourself), it's easier to find acceptance and compassion when you recognize that we only know what we know. Each of us is growing in love, but we haven't mastered complete unconditional love yet. We've got mind stuff to release first. We'll all get there eventually.

The More Evolved the Soul, the More Challenging the Lesson.

When your mind resists something or someone that your soul has deliberately brought to you, that's a clue as to what you have yet to master. What you resist will persist and grow until you are no longer triggered into negativity or fear by it. What or who you see as a challenge is designed as a motivator for growth. Once you use the uncomfortable experiences as an opportunity for soul growth, then they are no longer needed.

For instance, if your soul intends to obtain a Ph.D. in Acceptance in this particular incarnation, your lifetime "course curriculum" will center around acceptance. The more evolved you are as a soul, the more challenging the circumstances and people you will need to accept. You'll need to experience what acceptance is and isn't to gain mastery of it. You will need to accept such things as the spouse who watches too much violent TV, sharing a planet with people who have no respect for nature and animals, etc.

It is *important* to remember that it's not about what *they're* doing but what *you're* doing. They provide you with opportunities to respond from your heart instead of your conditioned mind. They are operating at their level of evolvement, but what about you? Are you reacting as a more advanced soul, with compassion and acceptance? Or are you responding from your egoic mind, with judgment and criticism?

Next, we will discuss your soul's choice of family members.

> *"Understand that everyone here on Earth is learning just as you are . . . and not everyone learns at the same pace or even the same lessons as you."*
> —Author Unknown

Day 25

The Stronger the Emotional Attachment, the More Potential for Soul Growth.

One of the toughest things to endure is watching a loved one make poor choices. Their choices may have disastrous consequences and make their lives more difficult. It's painful to witness. You want to take control of the situation and rescue them. If they're adults, that's not the best approach.

On a soul level, your spouse, son, daughter, mother or father may have chosen to become a drug addict and/or alcoholic to experience powerlessness and abuse of their body. They are providing you with opportunities to engage in deeper levels of non-judgment, compassion and acceptance. You have agreed on a soul level to not judge them but to accept their choices and unconditionally love them. You are here to love them while they learn to love themselves. No easy feat but you're up to the task.

We are conditioned to have expectations and beliefs of what family members *should* be like and how they ought to behave, especially toward us. The reality is that family members often *aren't capable* of measuring up to society's expected behavior.

If you are learning about acceptance, you may have a soul contract with your daughter who is emotionally distant from you. You may have a soul contract with your critical unloving father to help you master self-love. If your soul wants you to achieve greater levels of forgiveness, you may have soul contracts with your siblings, who have stolen part of your inheritance due to greed.

Family Members Have Soul Contracts to Play Different Roles in Each Other's Lives.

Sure, they could be making healthier, more loving choices, but there are no "right" or "wrong" decisions. They are going to learn from whatever choices they make, *especially* the painful ones. If they were evolved enough to make better choices they would have, but they aren't there yet. Even though it looks like they aren't "getting it," on a deep subconscious level they will carry that knowledge forward into future lifetimes.

Despite your mind's burning desire to fix things and need for change, it's best to remind yourself that you are souls who have deliberately chosen to be in the same family. You have soul contracts between you where everyone has agreed to play different roles in each other's lives.

Is there a family member whose choices you disapprove?

Next, we discuss the best way to handle the most challenging family member.

> *"Important encounters are planned by the souls long before the bodies see each other."*
> —Paulo Coelho, popular author

Day 26

Don't Do Your Loved One's Soul-Growth Homework.

You don't have control over people's behavior. You do have power over your response to them, though. Become aware when your mind is judging them and their behavior. The problem isn't with them, it's with your judging them.

You don't have to get stuck in their soul growth. When you change your response, you remove that "Velcro." There's no stickiness from your side, so you don't catch their issues.

Pay attention to what triggers you and why. Are you trying to stop loved ones from experiencing pain? Pain is a powerful teacher and motivator. They may need to descend into even deeper depths of depression and despair before they are ready to make needed changes. They may be releasing karma. You don't know the bigger picture. Don't do their soul-growth homework for them.

The Most Challenging Family Members May Be the Greatest Blessings in Your Soul Growth.

Honor the choices and lessons of others, rather than becoming dragged into a negative probability. What matters is how *you* respond to their behavior, not *their* actions. You are at a different stage of soul evolution than they are, and you are likely more advanced as a soul. Again, not better than—but you have more growth under your belt.

They are providing you opportunities to respond from your heart rather than your mind. Is your fearful mind reacting with judgment, intolerance, and anger? Or are you responding from your heart with acceptance, compassion and unconditional love? They are purposely in your path to help *you* grow.

You don't have to like their choices but at least accept them. Aim for neutrality—not affected one way or another, or pulled in emotionally. It's not about condoning harmful behavior. It also doesn't mean you have to expose yourself to toxic situations. That's a lesson right there about self-love. Protect yourself by setting limits and healthy boundaries with them.

This is not about rescuing anyone. It is about honoring their choices for their soul growth in their own way and at their pace. When your adult son uses alcohol and drugs to numb himself from a painful divorce, your role isn't to judge him. You likely have a soul contract to unconditionally love him while he learns to love and honor himself.

You'll find inner peace when your mind stops resisting family members that your soul has chosen for you. Recognize the gift your most challenging family members give you. Because of them this may be the lifetime you finally master acceptance, forgiveness and unconditional love.

Ask your angels and guides to help you find acceptance with challenging family members.

Next, we explore how you can find peace no matter what others are doing.

> *"Inner peace begins the moment you choose not to*
> *allow another person or event to control your emotions."*
> —Pema Chodron, international best-selling author

Day 27

We Are All *Equal* Souls at Different Stages of Development.

These are challenging times. We face extinction. Despite scientific data and increasing catastrophic events, many (especially those in power) refuse to admit our planet faces serious threats of climate change with devastating effects. Genocide, war and violence continue to rage. Drug addiction soars at epidemic levels. Our clean water supply is under unprecedented threat.

How do you find peace amidst the increasing devastation and chaos? One word: Perspective. You've got to see through the illusions and remember what's really going on. Awaken to the bigger picture.

It's helpful to keep in mind who you are and *why* you're here. You are a soul in a human body who bravely incarnated on this primitive planet. You chose Earth because it's a free-will planet with extreme contrasts of darkness and light. The extreme contrasts provide a limitless potential to make huge leaps in soul growth.

When everything is in perfection, as it is on the other side of the veil, it is stagnant for growth purposes. Growth is the name of the game for a soul. We develop much faster here through exploration and experience. It's easier to develop compassion when you've walked in someone else's shoes and suffered their hardships firsthand.

Earth offers a wide variety of diversity that comes in many forms. There are younger souls who tend to be violent, self-serving, greedy and materialistic. There are older, evolved souls who are compassionate, non-judgmental, loving and have a desire to be of service. There's also everything in between. We are all equal as souls, just at different stages of our development.

I'm not condoning malicious behavior. I am saying *accept* that everyone is at different levels of their development. Those in the earlier stages of soul growth don't know any better.

Respond from Your Heart, not Your Fearful Mind.

Everyone not only agreed to play certain roles in each other's lives but to go through specific experiences. On a soul level, the victims of a mass shooting volunteered to be injured or killed. The wildlife agreed to experience the horrific effects of a deadly oil spill or wildfire. A child abuser and the molested child consented to their circumstances before they incarnated.

Everyone and everything serve a purpose in our growth and development. It takes a lot sometimes to wake us up and open our hearts. That is where we are right now globally.

Be tolerant with the choices of others rather than being dragged into negativity and fear. You are at a different stage of soul evolvement than they are. Practice acceptance rather than judgment.

Acceptance does not equate to apathy. If you feel drawn to support organizations helping end inequality, do so. Just react from your heart not from a fearful mind desperately trying to control things. Fighting fear with fear never works. When you push, they push back.

People have developed into who they are for a reason. Dig a little deeper to understand the circumstances that molded them. Has love been withheld or withdrawn from them to make them behave the way they do? Compassion is easier when you're aware of what they've had to face or overcome.

Focus on the good in them and accept them exactly as they are. Find things to be grateful for about them, including the growth opportunities they present to you. When you have compassion and acceptance, you've passed the lesson.

Ask your angels and guides to help you find acceptance and peace with younger souls.

In the next lesson you will learn what happens when you ask angels and guides to help someone.

> *"Life will give you whatever experience is most helpful for the evolution of your consciousness."*
> —Eckhart Tolle, spiritual teacher, best-selling author

Day 28

When you ask angels and guides to help others, they
are allowed to assist by downloading love into them.

Angels *Always* Send Love Upon Request.

Although we want angels and spirit guides to help our loved ones, they will not intervene unless your loved one asks them for assistance. Angels and guides will never interfere with free will. They will help those who ask for help themselves. The reason, beyond free will, is that angels and guides understand the soul's lessons behind your loved one's difficulties.

If your daughter is addicted to shopping and deeply in debt, it may be her soul's intention for her to understand simplicity. She may need to experience bankruptcy before she is willing to release her need for fulfillment through material things.

In certain circumstances, angels and guides are allowed to help a child upon someone else's request. However, whenever you ask angels and guides to help someone over the age of 18, the one thing they will *always* send is love. That is a good thing. Put those *millions* of unemployed angels to work!

It is a great idea to ask angels and spirit guides to send love to:

- Your recently widowed friend and all those grieving

- Everyone struggling with financial insecurity

- All those discriminated against

- Wildlife struggling with the loss of habitat

- Every human and creature being abused

- Refugees and those living in war-torn areas

- Gaia and all her creatures

- The homeless

The possibilities are endless. Don't underestimate the power of love.

Get in the habit of enlisting angels and guides to send love to others while you are waiting in traffic or at a red light, in the shower, making your coffee . . . There is a tremendous need in the world for love. You bring more love to this planet and all those upon her by engaging angels and guides to send the energy of love out widely.

Next, we discuss how your deceased loved ones can actively remain in your life.

> *Upon your request, the angels and guides will send love to yourself and others.*

Day 29

Your departed loved one may choose to communicate with you.

Departed Loved Ones Remain Aware of Your Daily Life.

Upon physical death, the soul leaves the body. When crossing to the other side, they will be first greeted by their guardian angel(s), followed by their deceased animal companions, and finally, their departed loved ones. It is a joyous reunion and a homecoming.

Having shed the physical body and now resting on the other side of the veil, their vibration dramatically rises. Like a spinning airplane propeller, they usually are unable to be seen by earthbound beings.

In this higher-vibrational etheric state from the other side, your loved ones are still able to see and hear you as you go about your daily life. They can visit us on Earth and interact with the living if they choose.

Your deceased loved ones like to be here in spirit for significant events such as weddings, birthdays, holidays, births and deaths. They often remain a part of your life. They are aware of what is happening and will sometimes serve as a type of spirit guide for you.

Deceased Loved Ones Manipulate Energy to Get Your Attention.

The spirit world communicates through telepathy, so they are aware of your thoughts and feelings. Like the angels and spirit guides, your deceased loved ones can bilocate—they can be in several dimensions at the same time. When you call to them, you are not bothering them or keeping them from something else because of their bilocation abilities.

Your departed loved ones can communicate with you in ways similar to the angels and spirit guides (See Days 13 and 14.) One of the most common ways for deceased loved ones to communicate with us is through dreams.

These dreams are different than your usual dreams. You retain the memory of them.

Our deceased loved ones are energy. We are energy, too. As energy, our passed loved ones might manipulate it like turning on and off the computer, TV, radio, appliances, and lights. Maneuvering energy is one of the most effective ways of getting your attention.

They can also use their energy to be with us through animals, birds, and insects such as butterflies, ladybugs and dragonflies. If an animal or bird hangs around your yard, stares at you through a window or squawks at you, it could be your loved one conveying their presence. Your departed loved one is not the animal, bird or insect. They are using them to convey their messages to you.

Your departed loved ones are not trying to scare or harm you. If you do get scared by their means of communication, ask them to stop or tone it down. They are conveying their presence and are here to help you. Tell them how they can be of assistance.

Have you ever had a departed loved one communicate with you?

Next, we explore why your soul specifically chose a family lineage for you.

> *"What we often fail to realize is that even though a dead person's body is gone, their spirit is not. Their soul lives, not just in heaven but on earth."*
> —Bill Philipps, author, psychic medium

Day 30

You May Have Incarnated into a Specific Family Lineage to Heal Genetic Predispositions.

Sometimes older souls deliberately choose to incarnate into a family with a history of suffering from emotional ailments to end the genetic predisposition. Experiences are passed on through DNA. For instance, we retain our ancestors' fears through cellular memory.

You may have a family history of depression and suicide from your paternal ancestors. Your soul may have chosen this family heritage for you to experience paralyzing depression and then heal it. By healing your depression, you free past ancestors and future descendants.

Let me describe some scientific studies to help you understand this better. Scientists conducted studies on mice to determine whether we carry our ancestors' experiences in our cellular memory, our DNA. The scientists knew the mice loved cherries and almonds, so that became the basis for clinical experiments.

While the lab mice smelled the scent of either cherries or almonds, lab assistants would administer electric shocks to them. Even when the mice stopped being electrically shocked, they understandably became extremely anxious whenever they smelled cherries or almonds.

Through these studies, scientists discovered that *all* future descendants of the electrically shocked mice *also* had intense anxiety whenever they smelled cherries or almonds. The fear existed even though they had never experienced being electrically shocked themselves.

If you have a family history of depression, you may have deliberately chosen this family lineage to finally heal depression. You are now evolved enough as a soul to completely heal this depression. You also have all the help you need from the other side of the veil. The angels and spirit guides are waiting for you to allow them to assist you.

Next, we study how older souls take on the challenge of self-love.

> *"When we meet real tragedy in life, we can react in two ways—either by losing hope and falling into self-destructive habits, or by using the challenge to find our inner strength."*
> —Dalai Lama

Day 31

All negativity, criticism and judgment toward
yourself and others is childish and immature.

Your Soul Carefully Chose Circumstances to Help You Master Self-Love.

Older, advanced souls will often take on mastering greater self-love. Your soul may choose a disfigured body with a physical disability which embarrasses your mother. Your soul may choose to be gay in a deeply religious family which is antagonistic toward homosexuals.

Your soul may choose to be born dyslexic in a dirt-poor Hispanic family. Your soul may choose to be born African American in the ghettos of the inner city. Your soul may choose to be indoctrinated in a religion that is despised and discriminated against.

Since this journey is about developing self-love, you needed to experience circumstances that deliberately lead you to believe you are flawed and unworthy. From an early age, you will be led to believe you are "less than" and unlovable. Your mind will believe these distortions and misperceptions. Your mind will feed you negativity, criticism, judgment and comparisons to others. Your mind will abuse you. You will believe all the lies and withhold love from yourself.

It is time to heal by remembering who you are: an extraordinarily brave, glorious, Divine, luminous being. *Even though it is rampant in our society, all negativity, criticism, and judgment toward yourself (and others) is childish and immature.* It needs to stop *now*. Do not allow your abusive mind to take over and feed you lies. Instead of thinking, *I'm not good enough*, recognize this: *I'm having a* thought *which is telling me I'm not good enough.*

This lifetime is about controlling your mind rather than your mind controlling you. It begins with awareness. When your mind is feeding you negativity, stop and redirect it to more loving and supportive thoughts.

Over time you will gain awareness of the distorted beliefs and mindsets you've been carrying around. If you want to clear out a tree, it is best to take the whole tree down at once rather than to pull off one leaf at a time. If you want to clear out self-hatred, it is best to eliminate the sabotaging mindset at once rather than one thought at a time. Become aware of what false mindsets you have been led to believe about yourself which create dislike or self-hatred. As you release these falsehoods, you will slowly begin to fall in love with yourself.

What do you criticize about yourself?

Next, we will discuss why we mistakenly believe our angels and guides are not responding to our requests.

> *"What a liberation to realize that the 'voice in my head' is not who I am. What am I then? The one who sees that."*
> —Eckhart Tolle, spiritual teacher, best-selling author

Day 32

Your Frustrations with Angels and Guides Can Be Due to Unrealistic Expectations.

Do not get frustrated if you feel angels and guides do not hear you and are not responding to your requests. They hear your every request. They will respond in a timely fashion.

Possibly your mind is challenged by this concept of communicating with, and receiving help from, angelic beings and spirit guides. Maybe you are struggling with the belief that you have asked for help from angels in the past and they never responded before, so why would they now? This is a common response and perfectly understandable.

Perhaps you are discouraged that you are not noticing any signs from them. Despite your best efforts to focus you may be unable to see, hear or feel the presence of angels and guides. You may have difficulty trusting yourself and them.

Communicating with angels and guides is much like developing a new skill or sport. It is a little awkward at first. It is a process that requires practice and patience. Eventually you will recognize their signs better and understand their messages more clearly.

Everyone is clairsentient where you *feel* their guidance. Very few people have the ability to see (clairvoyant) or hear (clairaudient) angels and guides. It is unlikely you will feel their presence.

What you *will* feel is a sense of knowing, a physical sensation like goosebumps or tingling. You will experience a gut feeling, like a sinking in your stomach. As you develop your intuition (see Day 16), your capacity to identify their signs and understand their guidance will greatly improve.

It is reassuring to know that you are programmed to be intuitively guided by a higher consciousness. It was intended you would utilize assistance from a higher consciousness throughout your entire life.

It is incredibly easy for angels and guides to hear and help you. It is their joy to do so. If you miss their guidance, they will continue to send signs until you clearly understand the message. Getting their guidance across to you is *never* a problem.

What you probably need to do is release all expectations. Let go of "How?" and "When?" Sometimes there is divine timing involved. Other times angels and guides are restricted by your soul's intentions, and by Universal and Spiritual Laws.

You may have asked your angels and guides to help you stay employed during a company layoff. Your spirit team always honor free will and will never force anyone to do anything including your boss. Despite their best efforts, your employer decides to lay you off. Angels and guides then shift to Plan B (or Plan C or Plan D or Plan . . .) to find you a more appropriate, fulfilling job that fits your soul's goals.

Trust that you are loved more than you can comprehend. Angels and guides have your best interests at heart. They are quietly and persistently working in the background to fulfill your requests according to your soul's intentions.

Ask your angels and guides to help you develop more trust, patience, and a stronger intuition. Ask them to improve your ability to recognize their signs and interpret their messages.

Next, we explore how to manifest your desires.

Although the angels and guides respond to each
request, it may not be according to your desires.

Day 33

Meditation is a powerful tool. The world has become an increasingly stressful place, and developing a meditation habit can relieve anxiety and decrease stress.

Most People Habitually Think About What They Fear.

The benefits of meditating and easy ways to meditate were covered on Days 17-20. The benefits are so extensive that it is worth repeating words of encouragement to develop a daily meditation practice. Learning how to control your thoughts is essential to healthy living. That is why meditation has been increasingly growing in popularity worldwide.

Meditation trains the mind to be quiet by pushing the "pause button" on your incessant thoughts. This allows you to more easily feel the inner guidance from your soul, angels, and guides. By quieting your mind and tapping into your inner wisdom, you become an incredibly powerful self-healer and manifest more.

Meditation helps you quiet the mind's noisy habitual chatter, so you consciously shift from sabotaging, negative, fear-based thoughts to supportive love-based thoughts. Instead of wallowing in depression, think about what makes you grateful. Instead of focusing on what's lacking in your life, think about the abundance you have such as your health, intelligence, loving children, full cupboards, etc. Instead of continually replaying the morning's scenario where you and your partner argued, focus on the dozens of things that went right.

To be clear, I am not advocating a head-buried-in-the-sand type approach. What I am suggesting is that you focus on what you *want* rather than what you *don't want*. Our minds are incredibly powerful creators. Where your attention goes, energy flows, and that's what you ultimately draw to you and create. Most people spend their day obsessively mulling over and over in their minds what they *do not want*. Become mindful of what you're regularly thinking about, and whether it is sabotaging or supportive.

Here is a quick and easy meditation.

Find a quiet place and get in a comfortable seated position if possible. You can use nature for a stronger connection. Sit by the water's edge, lean against a tree, walk barefoot on the grass.

Place your attention inside the very center of your body. Feel the peaceful stillness and quiet there. Focus on the steady beating of your heart.

As thoughts drift into your mind, gently sweep them away like clouds.

Shift your attention for the next few minutes to thinking of something or someone in your life for which or for whom you are grateful.

Next, imagine inhaling a healing golden light throughout your entire body and exhaling your anxieties out.

End your meditation by grounding, where you imagine your feet growing roots into the earth like a tree.

It was a successful meditation even if you were only able to still your mind for a minute at a time. Any regular meditator will tell you that controlling your thoughts is a lifelong journey. Developing the habit of consciously shifting them to what supports you is worthwhile.

Is what you tend to obsess about really what you want to create in your life?

The next lesson deals with how to stop sabotaging thoughts.

"Meditation is like a gym in which you develop the powerful mental muscles of calm and insight."
—Ajahn Brahm, popular Buddhist teacher

Day 34

You Can Turn Sabotaging Thoughts into Supportive Ones— No Matter How Hard You've Tried Before.

If you are continuing to dwell in guilt, fear, anger, and negativity, it's time to stop the abuse of your mind. If your mind takes over and you become a slave to your thoughts, it's important to retrain your brain to respond in a supportive fashion. When you remain sad because you believe you've made mistakes (failed marriages, alcoholism, diabetes from food addiction, etc.), it's time to stop the internal beatings and recognize why you have gone through certain experiences.

You may realize you often think sabotaging thoughts, but you don't know how to turn your strong-willed mind around. Your mind may tell you: *It's too hard. I've always been this way. No matter what I do, I can't seem to change.*

However, there is tremendous hope. You aren't going to be doing this alone. Now you will be engaging tremendous help from angels and guides. That's a game changer. That takes it from 5 amps of power to 5,000 amps of power.

Here is the first step to turn things around once and for all.

1. **Observe your negative thoughts.** Become aware of *what triggered them.* Are you comparing yourself to others? Are you tired or hungry? Is there a distorted mindset involved? Do these thoughts stem from your mother, father, societal programming, a wounded or scared inner child?

Instead of being instantly emotionally dragged into negative thinking, *pause and observe*. It's become a habit to automatically be pulled into your mind's misperceptions. It's time to stop being battered by your mind's whims.

Realize that it was essential for your soul's journey to go through what you misperceive as "mistakes." You needed to experience several broken marriages or addiction as part of your soul's plan to help you grow and evolve. It was also your soul's intention to incarnate into a family with a distorted belief system so that you could overcome and heal.

It's not a good idea to compare yourself to others because everyone is on a unique path, determined by their soul's desires. If you are on a spiritual path, your life will be different than the mainstream, especially with regard to money and material possessions. As an older soul, you realize money is simply a tool.

When you are too tired or hungry, you are especially vulnerable to the negativity of your mind. That's when doubt, anxieties, and criticism creep in. Never allow your mind to step up on the "soapbox with a microphone" at the end of the day when you are tired, especially in bed. That's just asking for trouble.

There is often a misguided falsehood behind negative thinking. Maybe you were raised to believe your needs were not as important as others, so you feel guilty whenever you take time for yourself. Another lesson in self-love.

And by the way, never allow your mind to tell you *It's too hard to change.* Shift your thoughts to *Thanks for sharing but I'm not buying it.*

We continue the process in the next lesson.

"The moment you start watching your thoughts, a higher level of consciousness becomes activated."
—Eckhart Tolle, spiritual teacher, best-selling author

Day 35

Once you become aware of how fearful thoughts trigger you, you are more capable of redirecting them. You can transform negative thoughts into love-based ones.

Retrain Your Mind One Thought at a Time.

Once you have become aware of what triggers you into negativity, and whose voice is behind those thoughts (Step 1 as outlined in Day 34), it is time to move on to the next steps.

2. **Feel the emotion**. It is important to feel the emotion created by your negative thoughts. You never want to suppress feelings. Repressing negative emotion often leads to disease. More on that later. Allow the feelings to rise to the surface but do not "marinate" in fear or negative emotions for too long.

3. **Let it go**. Once you have felt the emotion derived from negative thinking, then let it go, let it go, let it go. It is as easy as hanging up on a toxic conversation or pressing the "mute" button. Although you are in the habit of engaging with these unhealthy thoughts, it does not mean you need to continue to do so.

4. **Redirect all negative-based thoughts and emotions to love-based ones**. I had a dog named Checkers who was extremely devoted to our family and always wanted to be right in the middle of whatever we were doing. In his canine mind, Checkers was convinced he was enormously helpful, even when he wasn't.

One winter, a massive evergreen tree crashed through our bedroom ceiling during a bad storm. During the repairs, Checkers was in everyone's way. Even though he was a nuisance, Checkers was confident he was helping.

If I locked Checkers out of the damaged bedroom, he would bark and scratch at the door, making matters worse. He desperately wanted to help. Checkers

72

needed to be involved in a helpful way, so I had him guard the front door and alert us when the workers arrived. Checkers was happy because he was participating and knew how to be a guard dog.

Checkers needed to be redirected, reassigned to a helpful assignment. In our family, when you think you are helping but you aren't—like clearing the dishes away before someone is finished eating—we call that "Checkers helping."

You are often on autopilot. Be more conscious and mindful. Our minds are extremely powerful, so it is important to become aware of sabotaging thoughts and steer them into thoughts that support what you want. Your Checkers-helping mind desperately wants to be involved, but it needs to be redirected. Reassign your mind a task that is helpful rather than one that creates havoc.

One thought at a time, retrain your mind to shift out of old Checkers-helping programming of negativity, judgment, and criticism into patience, kindness, and compassion. Gratitude will always serve you well in any instance. Can you find gratitude for how a challenging situation is helping you grow? Maybe you are learning in this lifetime what normally takes several.

Is what your mind telling you the truth or is it a lie? Just because you *think* something, does not mean it's true. It is simply a thought. Thoughts and feelings continually come and go.

Is your mind taking you through dark alleys of the past or the future? Almost everyone constantly relives memories of the past and indulges in imagining the future, but that is very unhealthy. It is a habit, and habits can be changed.

Bring your thoughts back to the present moment. That is where your power is, because that is where you create, and the present moment is all there is. The bigger the crisis, the more you need to keep your mind in the present moment.

Are unreasonable expectations creating negativity? Are you resisting what your soul has placed on your path? It's there for a reason.

Next, we will discuss the remainder of the process.

> *"Let go or be dragged."*
> —Zen proverb

Day 36

This Process Will Greatly Impact Your Life.

After following steps 1-4 as outlined in Days 34-35, use the remaining steps to break free from your mind's sabotage and finally reach your goals.

5. **See your goal already achieved.** Engage your formidable mind and imagine your goal is already accomplished. What does that look like? How does it feel? As you move in that direction emotionally and physically, the universe responds and moves that way, too.

6. **Hand your goal over to angels and spirit guides.** Engage the assistance of your angels and guides to help you attain your goal. Relinquish your mind to watch for their guidance. Release "How?" and "When?" this desired outcome will be attained.

7. **Follow their guidance with your gut instinct, intuition or sixth sense.** Guidance from angels and guides is based on love. You intuitively feel their guidance and what their messages mean. Guidance from your mind is fear-based. Your mind will tell you that you *should,* you *have to,* or you *need to.* Here is the ultimate guiding question: What would love do? Sometimes love sets up boundaries out of self-love.

8. **Ask your angelic team for additional help.** While angels and guides are helping you achieve your desired goal, ask them for assistance with anything else you need. Patience? More trust?

9. **Focus *only* on what you want**. There is a popular quote: *Mother Teresa would never attend an anti-war rally. She would only attend pro-peace events because she never wanted to give* any *energy to the war*. Remain focused on what you *want*. Don't give any energy or attention to what you *don't* want.

For instance, you do not say, "Thank you, angels and guides, for helping me get rid of this depression." Instead, what you say is, "Thank you, angels and guides, for helping me feel happiness and joy."

10. **Stay focused on imagining your goal already accomplished.** Remain focused on your desired result already achieved but be open to alternative outcomes. Angels and guides know what your soul intends and what is in your best interest.

This is a process which requires patience and practice. You will eventually get better at it. Be kind and gentle with yourself throughout the process.

Next is a summary of the 10-step process.

"We hold the key to our own happiness, but angels guide us to the right doors."
—Author Unknown

Day 37

> *You can achieve your goals with greater ease by engaging
> your powerful mind and assistance from angels and guides.*

Summary of 10-Step Process to Utilize Your Powerful Mind, Angels and Guides to Reach Any Goal:

1. **Observe your negative thoughts.** Become aware of what triggered them. Rather than automatically react with negativity, pause and observe. Recognize whose voice and what misperceptions led to those negative thoughts.

2. **Feel the emotion.** Feel the emotion that arises from those thoughts. You never want to suppress negative emotions because that often leads to disease. Allow the feelings to rise to the surface.

3. **Let it go.** Once you feel the emotions caused by negativity, let the thoughts and feelings go. Although you may have a habit of engaging with these unhealthy thoughts, you need to stop.

4. **Redirect all negative-based thoughts and emotions to love-based ones**. Reassign your Checkers-helping mind from fear, negativity and sabotaging thoughts into more love-based, supportive ones. Find gratitude. Keep your mind in the present. Discern whether your mind is telling a lie.

5. **See your goal already achieved.** Engage your imagination to envision your goal accomplished.

6. **Hand your goal over to angels and spirit guides.** Ask for help, and release the "How?" and "When?"

7. **Follow their guidance with your gut instinct, intuition or sixth sense.** Guidance from your angels and guides is love-based and feels right. Guidance from your mind is fear-based and tells you that you should, need to and have to.

8. **Ask your angelic team for additional help.** While they are assisting you with your desired goal, tell them what else you need help with.

9. **Focus *only* on what you want.** Remain focused on what you *want*. Don't give any energy or attention to what you *don't* want.

10. **Stay focused on your goal having already been accomplished.** Remain focused on your desired result already achieved but be open to alternative outcomes.

Next, we discuss how the mind, body, and soul are each equally involved in healing.

Angels and guides will empower you by
opening your mind to its greatest potential.

Day 38

*Our body is crumbling under the emotional
weight of our mind's negative emotions.*

Your Body, Mind, and Soul Are Equally Involved in Healing.

When it comes to healing, Western medicine and other popular healing modalities, sometimes miss the boat. They tend to address only the physical symptoms of an illness, ignoring two necessary elements to healing: the emotions and the soul.

The body, emotions, and soul are each *equally* involved in healing. When all three are in alignment, anything can be healed. *Anything!*

Your mind, body, and spirit are interconnected and not separate. Your physical body is a direct manifestation of the thoughts and emotions of your mind. To heal your body, you must address the needs of your soul and imbalances of your mind. Transformation and healing happen from the inside out.

Negative-Based Emotions Are Harmful to your Body.

There's nothing inherently wrong with any emotion. Every emotion serves a purpose. However, certain emotions have an unhealthy effect on your body.

Scientific studies have shown that 15 minutes of stress lowers your immune system for 24 hours. Negative-based emotions (i.e. fear, guilt, depression, frustration) create unhealthy cells, which overwhelm the system and become toxic. A build-up of these toxic emotions blocks the flow of energy, which leads to disease.

Negative emotions create cells that are very gunky and sticky, which clog and block the healthy life force flowing through you. Studies have proven that depression is a greater cause of heart disease than smoking. The blood platelets in depressed people are stickier, which clog arteries and veins.

Dr. Masaru Emoto's scientific experiments proved how each emotion forms a different type of cell which has a specific effect on the body. For instance, the emotion of grief produces a discombobulated "slacker" cell that is dense. It can't hold as much life-force energy (also known as prana or chi). Since a grief cell is heavier, it has a lower vibration, or lower frequency, which produces stagnant energy . . . a swampy mess perfect for the breeding of disease.

Emotions are held in specific areas of the body. We all tend to feel and hold grief in our chest area. You might unknowingly create a blockage in your chest if you are carrying a lot of grief. This could lead to a potentially dangerous situation, especially if you have heart disease or breast cancer in your family. Fibromyalgia often originates from unreleased fear held throughout the entire body.

Continually feeling negative emotions weakens your body. Shame, guilt and self-hatred are the hardest emotions for the body to process and cause the most damage. Your body can't thrive, let alone heal, under the heavy weight of negative emotions.

Fortunately, negative-based emotions and cells can be released through a variety of pleasurable activities such as laughing, meditation, walking, listening to music, etc.

Next, we discover how love-based emotions specifically affect your body.

> *When your body, emotions and soul are each*
> *aligned with healing, anything can be healed.*

Day 39

> *Your mind and body are intrinsically connected and*
> *dependent on one another. By taking control of your emotions,*
> *you can positively affect the healing processes of your body.*

You Heal Faster with Positive-Based Emotions.

Positive-based emotions have an entirely different effect on your body than negative-based ones. They create a chemical response which floods the body with beneficial neuropeptides such as endorphins or oxytocin.

Positive-based emotions (i.e. hope, forgiveness, joy, gratitude) create faster-vibrating, healthy cells which promote wellness by enhancing the flow of energy throughout the body. The result is like a flowing, thriving, vibrant "river" teeming with life energy. Disease cannot sustain itself in vibrant thriving cells.

Emotions that are love-based—positive—create a different type of cell which your body thrives on. Positive emotions such as gratitude emit a healing response throughout your entire body. When you feel gratitude, your body produces cells which are less dense and therefore able to hold more life-force energy.

Because gratitude cells are lighter, they vibrate faster, which causes a higher frequency or vibration—*vibrance!* In addition to gratitude, some of the best emotions to help you heal faster are love and forgiveness of others and self.

Your Brain Entrains with Your Heart's Electromagnetic Field.

Your heart generates a much greater electromagnetic force field than your brain. Your brain entrains with your heart's electromagnetic field, not the other way around. That means if your heart feels resentment, guilt or sadness, your brain will entrain with that and match its biological rhythm. Conversely, if your heart feels gratitude, forgiveness or happiness, your brain will entrain with *that* and move into a healthy vibratory pattern.

Next, we will discuss the emotional root cause of physical illness.

> *"… a person's mind exists in every part of his body, in every single cell. Because of this, every thought we have, each emotion we experience, has a physical effect upon our body."*
> —Dr. Gary Holz, physicist, psychoneuroimmunologist

Day 40

Negative Emotions Are the Root Cause of Disease.

Our emotions play a pivotal role in the disease process. Unhealthy feelings are often the root cause of our illness. For example, someone under a lot of stress may develop migraines or ulcers. These ill effects are not localized illness: they are rooted in emotion. Our thoughts and emotions create a healthy vibrant body . . . or disease.

You Need to Remove the Emotional Core of Disease to Sustain Healing.

You can see the importance of paying attention to what types of feelings you are engaging on a regular basis. It is a blessing to experience the full range of emotions that come with being human. But the trick is to not take them so seriously that you get stuck in quicksand with them. Emotional pain comes, you cry, that moment is over, and then you let it go. End of story. You don't want to set up shop or make a "movie trailer" about the things that happened.

Emotions are to be experienced, felt, learned from and released. You then move on to experience the next emotion which is felt, learned from, released, and so on. Remaining stuck in a negative-based emotion will create dis-ease; *disease*. When you dwell on certain situations with unhealthy feelings such as fear or criticism, you develop emotional and/or physical pain. If your emotions are uncomfortable, your body is being impacted.

While you never want to suppress any emotions, it is important to recognize that negative-based ones should not be engaged in longer than necessary. Here's why: We feel and hold resentment in our heart. Over time, if you feel bitterness toward your former spouse and don't release it, you will develop unhealthy cells and physical problems in your upper body. That's because this unreleased resentment creates a blockage of energy. Consequently, your heart chakra—which energetically recharges like a battery—will slow down and become unable to adequately deliver essential life-force energy throughout your chest.

Your unreleased bitterness is like a blinking dashboard light, warning you of a potentially hazardous situation. You ignore the warning and continue to immerse yourself in resentment daily. Eventually the dashboard warning light stays lit all the time. Now you have developed a physical problem—for example, a tumor in your left lung.

A skilled surgeon removes the tumor and gives an excellent prognosis. But you resume your old routines, including feeling bitterness toward your ex-husband. Eventually, doctors find a new tumor growing in your lung again. A tumor developed again because you didn't remove the underlying emotional core of unreleased resentment. Until you discover and remove this emotional core to your illness—unreleased resentment—you can't sustain healing from surgery, drugs or any other modality.

Next, we explore the role your mind plays in creating wellness or disease.

Your mind plays an important role in healing.

Day 41

> *You have the innate ability to heal.*

Your Mind Is a Major Factor in Well-Being or Disease.

You need the body, mind and soul each aligned with healing to be well and sustain any recovery. It is usually the body and soul that are in line with healing, but the mind, with its negative emotions, is not. Once you discover and release the emotional core to your illness, your mind comes into alignment with healing. At that point your body is able to restore itself and *sustain* that healing.

Since anyone suffering from an illness is in discomfort or pain, they tend to focus on the symptoms of their disease. They overlook the role emotions play in creating their disease. There is usually an emotional root to almost every illness. If you treat only the body and ignore the emotional core, it's like picking off the top of a dandelion. The illness will return because the emotional root is still there and has not been addressed.

You need to uproot all negative thoughts and emotions. Weed out fear-based, sabotaging mindsets and beliefs. Eradicate your mind's distortions and misperceptions. Gain awareness when you remain rooted in *any* negativity or fear.

Become cognizant of what type of emotions you regularly engage. They are either based on fear or love. Where are you getting emotionally stuck and why? There's your root.

Are you anxious over your daughter's alcoholism and unhealthy choices? It's likely you have a soul contract with her because you are enrolled in Acceptance 201 for your soul's growth.

Is your life unbalanced because you take care of everyone else's needs first and feel guilty when you nurture yourself? You may be immersed in a soul class on boundaries working toward your Ph.D. in Self-Love.

Do you berate yourself for the "mistakes" that resulted in three failed marriages? It's possible you signed up for soul master's classes in Self-Forgiveness.

Are you often upset because your spouse watches fear-based news? He is providing you with homework for your Acceptance class.

Do you ignore and neglect your body's needs? Looks like you are learning how to honor and respect the gift of your physical body as part of the Self-Love curriculum.

Is there a tape endlessly looping through your mind replaying your sister's constant criticism and the way she belittles you? She has a soul contract to help you master Forgiveness.

Are you frequently irritated by a coworker who is racist? He is deliberately in your path to help you obtain that Ph.D. in Acceptance (a popular degree with old souls).

Focus Only on What You Want.

Always focus on wellness as opposed to illness and its symptoms. The natural Law of Attraction says: *Whatever you focus on, you will attract.* Focus on healing by placing your attention on being well, not on the disease or pain. Create thoughts, feelings and beliefs centered on getting better. If you see yourself already healed, your body will likely move in that direction.

It's common to think healing is not happening. Healing is not linear. You do not get better and better and better. Sometimes it is two steps forward and one step back. Sometimes it is one step forward and two steps back . . . It takes time. Release expectations. Stay patient and be positive. You will get there.

Next, we will explore the important role the soul plays in healing.

Our bodies are continually removing
damaged cells and producing new, healthy ones.

Day 42

Anything can be healed when the body,
mind and soul are each aligned with healing.

The Soul's Voice Is Usually Overlooked in Illness.

Your soul's intentions are important in the healing process. Angels and guides are not allowed to help heal you if your soul is against it. If the soul is not aligned with healing, then there is a purpose behind that disease. Illness can sometimes be a way for the soul to get your attention and help you shift into healthier habits and thought patterns.

The sudden onset of the coronavirus has tremendous potential for increasing consciousness. After being diagnosed with COVID-19, you may awaken to the precious gift of life. You can find greater joy in the simplest things like the sound of your grandchildren's laughter, watching birds gracefully fly in formation, and the comfort of holding the hand of a loved one. Your heart becomes more open.

It is not uncommon for more advanced souls to take on greater physical challenges because they learn and grow more through adversity. For that reason, your soul may not agree to complete recovery from the debilitating effects of Parkinson's or Multiple Sclerosis. In some cases, though, the soul may agree to partial healing.

A baby born blind will have a life dramatically different than one with vision. Their other senses will become heightened and atypical perspectives gained. Blindness is necessary for that soul's journey and growth. Despite doctors' repeated attempts, the eyesight will never be restored, because the soul is not aligned with healing the blindness.

People may experience a painful disease to help them loosen their grip on this lifetime. Their soul is calling them home. In this instance, recovery will not occur because the soul—an essential component—does not support healing. Witnessing their loved one go through intense physical pain, family and friends eventually release them to physically pass. The painful disease served multiple purposes.

A *Sustained* Recovery Is Achieved *Only* When Body, Mind, and Soul Are Each Aligned with Healing.

For most people, their soul supports vibrant health, but we often create more pain and illness than our soul intended. It is our emotions that create a physical problem. It is likely that emotional and physical pain have finally gotten your attention.

How bad does it have to get before you are willing to listen to your soul's guidance? Your soul may be using the disease as a messenger to guide you in a different direction than the negative course you are taking.

In some instances, where your soul supports healing and you have finally gotten your emotions aligned, the disease may have become too advanced for your body to heal. In that case, the body is not supportive of healing. Angels and guides must follow Universal Laws and are unable to heal you.

Your body, mind, and soul are equal partners in the healing process. When they are each aligned with healing, sustained recovery and vibrant health are the outcomes.

How is a physical challenge helping you grow and evolve as a soul?

Next, we discuss how we misuse our mind.

A soul may use an illness for growth, but it will never use it as a form of punishment.

88

Day 43

You're Perfect *Exactly* the Way You Are.

We have discussed the concept of Earth being a school where you can make huge leaps in soul growth because of the extreme contrasts. We're all learning to control our thoughts, and shift from our egoic minds to our compassionate, loving hearts. One of our greatest challenges is to overcome the mind's misperception that we are broken and need to be fixed. In truth, you are exactly the way you need to be for what you are here to learn.

The Greater the Challenge, the Greater the Growth Potential.

Your life's journey is designed to help you gain awareness and release your mind's fears, limiting beliefs and distortions. Everyone and everything in your life is there by design, to help you break free from your mind's pain, negativity, and lies. There is an agreement to help you clean up any unhealthy emotional "dust bunnies."

When your mind resists something or someone that your soul has brought to you, that's a clue as to what you signed up to learn. What you resist will persist and grow until you're no longer triggered into negativity or fear by it.

Your soul places in your path what it wants your mind to grow beyond and master. *What you see as a challenge is a catalyst for growth.* Once you use these uncomfortable experiences as an opportunity for evolution, then they are no longer needed. Mission accomplished.

If you fear not having enough money, "pop quizzes" will continue until you realize that you have what you need. If you get angry at the choices people make, the triggers will continue until you accept that their decisions are part of their evolutionary path. It's not about what *they're* doing but what *you're*

89

doing. It's a great opportunity to choose whether to react from your judgmental mind or your compassionate heart.

Stop Resisting Growth Opportunities.

The majority of what is on your path is designed to promote growth. However, it was never intended for your mind to be behind the steering wheel, navigating you through your challenges. Your fearful, conditioned mind will lead you through all kinds of dark alleys because it doesn't know any better.

Your *soul* is supposed to be in the driver's seat. Your mind is a powerful tool to use in service to your soul. Your soul guides your mind with intuition, sixth sense, and gut instinct.

Your mind doesn't always like what your soul brings to you. It lashes out and grabs the wheel to steer you away from painful experiences and emotions. In response, you create unnecessary pain and struggle from fear, stress, resentment or anger. Your soul will then course correct to go through these necessary experiences.

The answer is to allow your soul to bring you what it knows you need for your growth (which it's going to do anyway). Instead of resisting, ask yourself: *Why is this on my path? How is this here to help me grow?* As your mind surrenders to what is, you gain consciousness as to where you've been stuck and need to make changes. When you have adjusted your thinking and behavior, you'll find greater peace and happiness. That is where your soul is leading you.

The next lesson will help you stop worrying.

> *When you replace "Why is this happening to me?" with "What is this trying to teach me?" everything shifts.*

Day 44

> *Worrying your way through any difficulty will do you no favors. The more of a crisis, the more you need to stop worrying and stay in the present moment.*

Persistent and Uncontrollable Worry Is a Problem.

Worrying is a normal part of life. Everyone does it to some extent. Excessive worrying can harm your emotional and physical health. Worrying rarely does any good. Yet, it's habitual for most people. Like any habit, it can be changed.

Postpone Worrying to a Specific "Worry Time."

It doesn't always work to tell yourself to stop worrying. You can distract yourself for a while, but it's like trying to ignore the pink elephant in the room. Your thoughts wander right back to the exact thing you want to forget. The increased attention makes your worries stronger and more persistent.

Instead of trying to stop or get rid of anxious thoughts, *postpone* worrying. Permit yourself to ruminate at a designated time when you aren't vulnerable (*never* around bedtime or when you're tired).

You're allowed to dwell on your anxieties *only* during your specified Worry Time in a focused and effective way. The rest of your day is worry-free. When worries creep into your thoughts, write them on your Worry List for later, and then continue with your day.

Recognize Worrying Is Harmful and a Waste of Time.

You need to understand that there's a difference between worrying and problem-solving. Worrying is a waste of time and energy. It doesn't change anything, but it is excellent at making you anxious and sleep deprived. Problem-solving involves working on solutions and is productive.

Distinguish between solvable and unsolvable problems. If what you're fretting about is unsolvable, accept the uncertainty. Life is unpredictable and a bit messy sometimes.

It does you no good to worry about things you can't control. You have no control over someone else's behavior or over events, but you can control your reaction. You'll be happier in life if you put your thoughts, time and energy into what you can control, and accept what you can't control.

Stay Focused on the Present Moment.

Rather than ignore or fight your worries, simply observe them. If you stop trying to control the anxious thoughts that arise, they will eventually pass. It's when you react and engage with your anxieties that you get pulled in and stuck. If you direct your attention to the here and now, the worries gradually disappear on their own.

It's harmful to mentally rehash things you've said or done in the past. It also doesn't help to agonize about the future. The "what-ifs" you create in your mind are usually much worse than what you feel when something does happen. It is also rarely as bad as you imagine it will be. These are all reasons why you need to stay in the present moment. You do that through mindfulness. Being mindful and present stops the endless rumination.

Shift 100% of your attention to what's going on within and around you. Feel your heart steadily beating in your chest, sense your clothing against your skin, and focus on your breath. Fully engaging in your surroundings and what's going on inside of you is an effective way to disrupt fretful thinking and produce a calming effect.

You Choose to Worry or Be Happy.

Accept that worrying is part of the human experience. It's a necessary element of the shadow self. Overcoming worry is part of the natural progression of learning how to control your thoughts rather than letting your thoughts control you. Who knows, maybe your soul deliberately wanted you to incarnate into a family who worry a lot. Ah, the conditioning you'd undergo is rich! It certainly provides tremendous growth opportunities in gaining control over unhealthy thoughts.

As Mark Twain wisely noted: "I've suffered a great many catastrophes in my life. Most of them never happened." It makes no sense to put yourself through unnecessary emotional anguish. Keep in mind that it's always your choice.

Ask the angels and spirit guides to help you find peace.

Next, we explore how to develop self-acceptance.

> *"Worrying is like a rocking chair. It gives you something to do but doesn't get you anywhere."*
> —Erma Bombeck, best-selling author

Day 45

> *Loving yourself is the absence of negative thoughts and judgment about yourself.*

Self-Acceptance Is Essential.

If you're having a hard time accepting certain parts of yourself, it's because it's not something you want. You're *exactly* the way you need to be for your soul's unique journey. You're extraordinary: a glorious, Divine, luminous being. Release your mind's misperceptions that the shadow parts of you are bad and need to be eliminated.

A painting is created with contrasts. Likewise, it's the shadow within you that provides contrast to the light so that you see things more clearly. Shadow is a partner to light and often necessary for soul growth. Stop demonizing the shadow with black-and-white thinking. Cherish it in you as much as you do the light.

Your Shadow Serves You.

We're *all* on the path of enlightenment about ourselves. We'll get there eventually. Shadow helps you navigate. If you want a detour or distraction from your soul's evolution, shadow will help you with that.

Your shadow says: "I've got things to keep you distracted—TV, busyness, food, laziness, Internet, judgments. Here's an excellent distraction—you don't deserve unconditional love. Play with that for a while." The design and execution of our distractions are breathtaking.

Your Egoic Mind Often Lies to You.

It's easier to have non-acceptance and resist what is when you compare yourself and your life to others. *You're on a different path.* Your spiritual journey doesn't fit in with the mainstream and isn't comparable. You can't be a person of depth without difficulty, pain, trauma, and disappointment. It's through these things that you find your magnificence.

Want to be a better friend to yourself? Stop the judgment. Don't strive for a perfect body. It's never going to be perfect. Don't set the bar too high for constant unconditional love. After all, we're in limiting bodies. Do, however, reach beyond your comfort zone.

Earth is like a university you're passing through. Your body is the "classroom." You have learning experiences through your classroom which help you evolve and grow.

How do you want to live? How much are you going to abdicate to your shadow or consciousness? You've stayed on the bench long enough. It's time to get up and challenge your shadow. Is what your shadow telling you true? Shadow likes vague, broad statements. Shadow doesn't like specificity. Use discernment, not judgment.

Self-Acceptance Is Developed through Practice.

The best time to practice self-acceptance is when you judge yourself. The next time you're criticizing yourself, pause and take two deep breaths. Go within your heart to find the compassion that rests there.

If the critical, judgmental voice starts up again, quiet it with a gentle internal "Shh" and take a few deep breaths. Listen within for the kind words you need. They will help you feel peaceful and accepted. Do this as often as necessary to make it a habit.

Your mind is a powerful tool. It's up to you to train and use it properly. Allowing it to stand in the way of accepting and loving yourself *just as you are* needs to stop. Now. What have you disliked about yourself that you are willing to at least accept now?

The next lesson deals with responsibility.

You are the way you need to be for your
soul's intended growth in this incarnation.

Day 46

> *You are in control of how you respond to life's difficulties.*

Responsibility Is a Learned Skill.

Responsibility doesn't just happen. It's determined by your choices. It's a skill. You learn it. A responsible person is one who can be trusted to tackle tough tasks without needing to be micromanaged. They are responsible for the consequences, whether that's failure or success. A responsible person is accountable for his or her behavior.

Be Honest When You Fail.

Don't make excuses. Coming up with an excuse is irresponsible. It's the "dog-ate-my-homework" mentality that keeps you a victim rather than one taking control of your life.

If you're late to the meeting, own up to it. Don't blame it on traffic. You simply didn't leave early enough for unpredictable traffic jams. Instead of placing the blame on someone or something else, be honest about why you failed. Be accountable for your actions.

Stop Unhealthy Coping Defenses.

Everyone develops coping mechanisms, starting as a child. To protect your-self from painful feelings you might develop psychological defenses such as avoidance, denial, suppression or an addiction.

What protected you as a child is likely now creating dysfunction and restrictions in your life. It's interfering with your ability to develop and mature as a responsible adult. Start becoming aware of the defenses that protect you from pain. Challenge them. Be willing to be vulnerable and uncomfortable — to feel life, even the yucky stuff.

96

Push Yourself to Do *At Least* One Small Task.

To develop responsible habits, it's helpful to start small. What small task can you accomplish and mark off your to-do list? If you have an overwhelming project, break it up into smaller pieces.

Once you get the momentum flowing, it gets easier. Sure, it takes an effort. You may have to force yourself up off the couch to make it happen but (and I hate to sound cliché) *just do it*.

Push yourself to do one small thing at a time. Make your bed. Make it again the next day. Throw in one load of laundry. One load of laundry! Straighten up one drawer or the corner of your desk. Eventually it gets easier and these things become habits. Bonus: You'll start feeling a lot better.

Prove You're Trustworthy.

It's one thing to let yourself down but it's quite another to be unreliable to others. Actions speak louder than words. If you've borrowed something, return it in good condition in a timely fashion. If you've told the hostess you'll bring dessert, make sure you show up on time with a dessert. Demonstrate that they can count on you once you've committed.

Being responsible doesn't mean random, haphazard or hit-and-miss. Consistency is the key. Responsibility requires you to *consistently engage in good habits*. Develop a regular routine and stick to it. Set your alarm and get up at the same time every day. Don't let emails pile up in your inbox until they are overwhelming. Spend a set amount of time every day handling emails.

Take Control of Your Life.

Being responsible means that you don't do things in a shoddy fashion or leave things half done. If you're given a job, do the best you can, see it through to the end, and own up to the outcome.

Being responsible means you're in control of your life, not a victim of circumstance. *You* are in control of what you do and don't do. Don't place the blame on anyone or anything else. Life will be better for it.

Ask your angels and guides to help you become responsible.

Next, we explore how we are shifting from the third dimension into the fourth and fifth dimensions.

> *"You cannot escape the responsibility of tomorrow by evading it today."*
> —Abraham Lincoln

Day 47

We Live in a Multidimensional Universe.

The Earth and most of her inhabitants are living a three-dimensional existence. Dimensions are not located in a specific place. They are degrees of consciousness that vibrate at a certain frequency. Each dimension vibrates at a higher frequency than the dimension below it.

In each higher dimension, there exists a greater level of knowledge and a clearer perspective of reality. The dimension you are a part of and your level of consciousness depends on the frequency you are vibrating at energetically.

We enter the next higher dimension when we vibrate in resonance with it. When you shift into the next higher dimension, it means you now vibrate at that level of consciousness, of awareness. You do not get pulled back into the lower frequencies.

While those living in a third, fourth, or fifth level of consciousness are experiencing the same reality, their way of perceiving it is completely different. You can experience multiple dimensions at the same time. You may have some belief systems still rooted in the third dimension while other viewpoints are embedded at a higher dimension.

Judgment and Fear Are Prevalent in the Third Dimension.

The fifth dimension is an energetic frequency band that vibrates higher than the third dimension we currently occupy. Our guardian angels, many of our spirit guides, and our deceased loved ones, vibrate at this fifth-dimensional level of consciousness.

Humans and the higher animal kingdom currently vibrate at a third-dimensional frequency. Here the level of human consciousness is extremely limited and restricted. We believe this is how "reality" is without realizing it is a very skewed perspective.

The third dimension operates on narrow beliefs. For example, you believe in duality, where you see yourself as separate from other people and the universe. You have belief systems where you judge people based on their gender, ethnicity, financial status, religion, appearance, etc. A person in the third dimension is energetically aligned with a slower vibration that holds third-dimensional viewpoints.

Higher Consciousness Begins to Awaken in the Fourth Dimension.

You are in the fourth-dimensional frequency when you vibrationally align with fourth-dimensional perspectives. You are in fourth-dimensional alignment, or energy, when you experience gratitude, joy or love. The fourth dimension is where some of us are now. Here we begin to awaken. As we move into higher consciousness, we realize the third-dimensional belief system is irrational.

The fourth dimension is all around us. You enter the fourth dimension when your mind is in an altered state of consciousness, which is sometimes reached through meditation.

Everyone Communicates through Telepathy in the Fifth Dimension.

The fifth dimension is the realm of love, where you respond from your heart and not your egoic mind. Someone in the fifth dimension is energetically aligned to the frequency with fifth-dimensional views. That means you have no negativity. None whatsoever. No fear, judgment, shame, hostility or guilt. There is no emotional suffering or belief in separation.

At this higher consciousness, you have gained mastery over your thoughts, which is imperative since when you think something, it instantly manifests. Telepathy is the main form of communication, allowing you to easily read other's thoughts. There is no distinction between the past, present or future. Our goal is to reach the fifth-dimensional consciousness. After we have reached the fifth dimension, we will continue to ascend into higher dimensions.

Angels and Guides Are Helping Us Become a Fifth-Dimensional Planet.

All beings on Earth are currently transitioning into a higher consciousness where compassion, love and peace prevail. Everyone is moving into these higher-vibrational states of consciousness at their own pace. When your vibration is high enough to match the frequency of the fourth or fifth dimensions, you gain a higher consciousness. You awaken to more advanced perspectives and find peace.

Hundreds of thousands of people worldwide are now experiencing an awakening into a higher consciousness at an unprecedented rate. As their vibration rises into love-based frequencies, they respond from the heart rather than the conditioned, egoic mind.

There is *unparalleled* assistance from the other side of the veil to help us rise into these higher frequencies so that we can become a planet of fifth-dimensional mentality, harmony and love.

Next, we discuss vibrations and how they affect you.

You ascend into the next dimension when your frequency matches the vibration of the higher level.

Day 48

> *Everything is energy.*

Energy Waves Attract Energy Waves of the Same Frequency.

You are a being of energy and light. Every single thought, emotion, being and thing is energy. Everything is energy! While objects may appear to be solid, they are extremely compacted energy particles creating a physical form. A molecule is either vibrating faster, which produces higher vibrations, or slower, which produces lower vibrations. Energy is never static or stagnant.

Your physical body is surrounded by emotional, mental and spiritual layers of energy. These different energetic layers combine to create your overall vibration. Every second you are either raising or lowering your vibration—constantly changing your frequency.

When you have a lower vibration, the light particles vibrate slower and become compacted. When vibrating at a reduced rate, you feel heavy, lethargic, negative emotions and have health issues. Distorted mindsets, guilt, judgment, addiction, anger, fear, greed, and ill health hold you down in dense, lower-vibrating energy.

When you have a higher vibration, you feel lighter, happier, and peaceful. You experience greater vitality, well-being, joy, creativity, stronger intuition, and love.

Your frequency level has a major impact on who and what you attract into your life. Like energy attracts like energy. When your vibration is higher, you attract people who are happier and loving. The higher your vibration, the faster you manifest your desires and better opportunities come to you. Lower vibrations attract negative people and toxic situations.

Higher Vibrations Increase Life-Force Energy and Light in Your Cells.

The higher your vibration and the more light you hold, the faster your light particles vibrate. High vibrational frequencies mean a higher consciousness and a stronger connection to your soul and Divine Source.

When you are a high-vibrational being, you recognize your divinity and the divinity within others. You are in alignment with your soul, which is nourished by Spirit. You are vibrantly healthy and your life flows with ease and grace. When your vibration is low, your energy feels heavy because you are not in alignment with your soul or divine self, and are operating from your lower self or ego.

By raising your vibration, you experience increased spiritual awareness because you are aligned more with Divine Source energy. The higher your vibration, the greater your consciousness and the more love you generate.

Dr. David Hawkins, an internationally renowned researcher, quantified the levels of vibration for different emotions. Enlightenment has the highest vibration, followed by peace, joy, and love. The emotion with the lowest vibration is shame, followed by guilt, grief, and fear.

Every thought, emotion, and choice affect your vibration. They also determine your ability to hold life-force energy and light in your cells. As you raise your vibration, you increase and retain more light. As you release negative emotions, sabotaging belief systems, and detoxify your body, the amount of life-force energy and light in your cells expands.

Ask your angels and guides to help you continually raise your vibration.

Next, you will learn what foods and activities raise and lower your vibration.

"Everything in life is vibration."
—Albert Einstein

Day 49

> *By making a conscious effort to raise your vibration,*
> *you will overcome fear, depression and anxiety.*

You raise your vibration with the way you think, feel and act. Employing any of the following suggestions will raise your vibration to varying degrees. Also listed are some of the ways your vibration is lowered.

Food and Drinks that Raise Your Vibration:

- Organic, unprocessed fruits and vegetables
- Natural and raw foods
- Spring or filtered water
- Herbal teas

Food and Drinks that Lower Your Vibration:

- Highly processed and animal products
- Chemically enhanced and genetically modified
- Junk and fast food
- Frozen
- Artificially sweetened
- Treated water, *especially* with fluoride
- Alcohol

Activities that Raise Your Vibration:

- Movement, such as dancing, walking, gardening, etc.
- Yoga, tai chi, qi gong, etc.
- Exercise

- Meditation
- Taking a detox bath (1 cup Epsom salt, 1 cup salt, ½ cup apple cider vinegar, combined)
- Using healing modalities like acupuncture, homeopathy and sound therapy
- Listening to uplifting or relaxing music
- Watching quality, lighthearted TV or movies
- Being creative
- Reading inspirational and positive books or multimedia
- Having fun
- Unplugging and relaxing
- Spending time with animals
- Keeping your environment clutter-free
- Being in nature

Activities that Lower Your Vibration:

- Sitting
- Smoking and vaping
- Using recreational and pharmaceutical drugs
- Watching violent or low-quality TV or movies
- Reading fear-based news
- Listening to harsh or abrasive music
- Playing violent video games
- Reading gossip in magazines or on multimedia
- Any addictive behavior
- Using toxic products

Next, we explore emotions and actions that raise and lower your vibration.

> *Angels and guides vibrate at a higher frequency. When we raise our energetic vibration, it is easier for us to receive their messages.*

Day 50

Emotions that Raise Your Vibration:

- Compassion
- Peace
- Joy
- Love
- Gratitude
- Acceptance

Emotions that Lower Your Vibration:

- Shame
- Guilt
- Grief
- Fear
- Desire
- Anger
- Pride
- Vanity
- Resentment
- Stress or anxiety

Actions that Raise Your Vibration:

- Acts of love

- Forgiveness
- Laughing
- Extending kindness
- Engaging in mindfulness
- Giving
- Anything in service to others
- Being patient
- Living in simplicity

Actions that Lower Your Vibration:

- Judging others and yourself
- Gossiping
- Negative self-talk
- Involvement with toxic people or relationships
- Complaining
- Surrounding yourself with clutter
- Neglect of self
- Selfishness
- Engaging in materialism

As you lift yourself into higher vibrations, you raise others around you. Like a tuning fork, your higher vibrations extend outward and lift the frequency of those surrounding you.

The angels and guides are excellent allies in increasing your vibration. Ask them to help you raise your vibrations so you can hold more light than ever before.

Next, we will discuss how to overcome any emotional trauma.

The higher your vibration, the more joy and peace you feel.

Day 51

Nobody Can Hurt You Without Your Permission.

Life can be especially challenging if you are haunted by your past. If you've been through a traumatic event(s), it can be difficult not to have scars. Your view of yourself and the world may be dramatically altered. Bitterness, shame or sadness may lie just beneath the surface, waiting to erupt. You *can* break free and move beyond trauma to enjoy a richer, fuller life.

Don't let the past define you. Take back your power, especially from those who have hurt you. You determine which stories you tell.

Take control of what you allow your egoic mind to say. You wouldn't let someone berate an emotionally wounded person. You certainly wouldn't put up with them spouting destructive things at someone already vulnerable. Don't allow your mind to beat you up, be critical or keep you small. Consciously shift your thoughts to be supportive, compassionate, kind and patient.

Physical Movement Can Be Your Best Friend.

Trauma disrupts your body's nervous system. It can keep you stuck in hypervigilance and fear. To get your body back into its natural rhythm and flow, you "unfreeze" it with physical activity. Try to exercise a total of at least 30 minutes a day. You'll start feeling better as the exercise releases adrenaline and emits endorphins.

You Control Your Reactions.

The human experience will naturally invoke suffering and loss. It's part of the package you signed up for. (Psst, it was in the really small print at the bottom of the last page). Remember *who* you are and *why* you're here. Your journey is deliberate about what you will experience and explore for growth. This lifetime is about exponential soul growth for you.

Your soul may want to master deeper levels of forgiveness in this lifetime. Or maybe this incarnation is to help you finally achieve greater acceptance, especially of other people's choices. You may be clearing karma from past lifetimes. Your mind may hate it, but your soul knows painful experiences can be growth "goldmines." You may have hit the mother lode.

You may not be able to control what happens or happened to you, but you can control your reaction to it. Are you going to react from your egoic mind with resentment, anger or guilt? Or will you let your heart respond with compassion, forgiveness, and love? One will help you move through painful events, while the other will keep you immersed in it so long as you are willing to allow it.

You choose whether to use these painful events as a place to set up camp, or as stepping stones to help you attain something better. After going through a painful divorce, you can remain stuck in negativity and fear of being in another relationship. Or you can use the experience to learn. Your choice.

Change the Story You Tell Yourself.

When you can't control what's happened to you, challenge yourself to control the way you respond to it. That's where your power lies. To heal from painful experiences, you've got to neutralize the story so that it loses its power and hold on you. See the experience as an opportunity to grow. Think: *How has it helped me evolve?*

Shift your perspective from victim to creator. Create a life where you transcend hardship. Create a life where you live in the moment. Create a life of gratitude.

Don't Give Your Past the Power to Define Your Future.

What's happened isn't going to change. Your perspective can shift, though. It will be the difference between feeling powerless and unhappy to being empowered, at peace, and joyful.

You become free of the past when you stop dwelling on it. There's a wise quote by C.S. Lewis: "Getting over a painful experience is much like crossing the monkey bars. You have to let go at some point to move forward." Let go of your "monkey bar," move on, and be happy in the now.

Ask the angels and spirit guides to help you release any painful circumstances(s), understand the reason it was in your life, and find peace.

Next, we discuss wisdom.

> *Never be a prisoner of your past. It was just a lesson, not a life sentence.*

Day 52

> *There are no "mistakes," only growth opportunities.*

Wisdom Will Help You Reach Higher States of Consciousness.

Who doesn't want to be wiser? To quote Confucius: *"By three methods we may learn wisdom. First, by reflection, which is noblest; second, by imitation, which is easiest; and third, by experience, which is the bittersweet."*

Acquiring Wisdom Is a Conscious Choice.

It's a myth that you need to be older and smarter to be wise. It's not about the number of life experiences you've been through. It's about the quality of reflection about your experiences. Developing wisdom is a deliberate choice which you make regardless of your age and intelligence. It will bring you greater peace, happiness, and clarity.

Those who are wise take the time to get to know someone rather than judge them on their appearance which can be deceiving. The wise person chooses to see others by their inner self, not who they purport to be. There is a difference. They also tune into their gut instinct, their intuition. The mind may be easily misled but intuition is not.

Wise people don't judge others. Instead, they practice empathy. Being empathic means putting yourself in their shoes and trying to see things from their perspective. It doesn't mean you agree with them, but you can see why they feel the way they do. The more you understand them, the easier it is to get a picture of why they are the way they are.

Learn from the Past and Move on *Without Regrets.*

We have been conditioned to believe that making a "mistake" is bad and seen as a failure. In truth, making mistakes are *necessary elements* to life, which

111

help us become wiser and reach our goals. Like a toddler learning how to walk, falls, bumps and bruises are part of the process. Mistakes and failings are rich opportunities to learn and grow. They guide us to know what to avoid, how to overcome obstacles, and the better direction to take.

Those who are wise learn from the past and then move on *without regrets*. They are not emotionally attached to the past. It's done. It's over. The wise don't allow their egoic mind to cling to what's passed. They don't live with shoulda, coulda, woulda. They are rooted in the present, the now, and the moment—that's what's important.

Self-Reflection Will Help You Acquire Powerful Knowledge.

In today's world, it's easy to get caught up in distractions and lose sight of what matters. You forget you're a Divine luminous soul, currently in a human body, with a mind that always wants to wander *everywhere*. However, what the egoic mind doesn't want to do is explore the inner self. The inner self is where true wisdom lies. It's your connection to an infinite source of eternal universal knowledge.

Throughout the ages, there are images of enlightened people meditating in quiet tranquil places. They understand that peace and clarity allow you to see your inner self more clearly. To do that you need to loosen your identification with the chatty mind and raise your consciousness by listening to the inner voice of your soul. Your soul's voice will reveal your deeper nature and profound wisdom.

Once you know who you are and realize your heart's desires, then you see more of the opportunities you failed to recognize before. This increased clarity will help you make better choices.

Question Traditional Beliefs.

Most people tend to go with the flow, while those who are wise will challenge the status quo. Wise people may question and doubt long-held beliefs, especially related to religion, politics, and philosophy.

Instead of accepting everything at face value, wisdom involves asking if that's true for you. Those who are wise will step back and re-evaluate commonly accepted norms and long-standing traditions. The wise do not follow the Pied Piper. They march to the beat of a different drum.

Being wise can save you a lot of pain, struggle, and heartache. You become wiser through experience, reflection and developing certain skills. Wisdom is available to all of us. The wiser we each become, the better the world at large will be.

Next, we will discuss how to find peace in the chaos.

"Knowing yourself is the beginning of all wisdom."
—Aristotle

Day 53

We are in the beginning stages of the biggest collective awakening ever seen in the history of mankind.

You Can Find Peace in the Chaos.

The world is engulfed in one crisis after another. Our planet appears to be heading toward disastrous consequences because we humans continue to foul our nest. Governments and economies around the world are crumbling. It's hard to not feel fearful and hopeless with all this chaos.-

What's important to keep in mind is there's a bigger picture at play here; things are not as they appear. Everything is happening exactly the way it is for a reason. Our planet is going through birthing pains. Gaia is becoming a *spiritual planet,* and that means change is necessary. Big change.

You chose to be here right now to help in these auspicious times as the planet shifts into higher consciousness. You came to help by increasing the energies of compassion, joy, and love. As you feel these emotions, their energies move through you and out into the world, adding to the collective.

Where attention goes, energy flows. Are you focusing on the darkness and chaos of the world? Or are you noticing the good in people and especially those making a positive difference? Are you envisioning our planet in despair and destruction or as a peaceful harmonic world?

There Are Many Reasons for Hope.

One of the best things you can do is make life-affirming, compassionate choices every day. That's worth repeating: *Make life-affirming, compassionate choices every day.* Do you buy organic eggs where the chickens are humanely treated, or mass-produced eggs from overcrowded, dismal conditions?

Your purchasing power has tremendous influence. It's important to support those who are good stewards of the Earth. Do you purchase the paper towels on sale or the ones that are eco-friendly? Simple everyday choices make a difference.

Around the globe people in *very large numbers* are quietly shifting into higher consciousness. They are remembering that we're interconnected.

When you have a higher consciousness, you think and act differently. You live from a state of love, with a strong desire to help those in need, with deep respect for our beloved planet and everything on her, and with acceptance of others. You'll discover greater consciousness all around if you look for it. You're not going to hear about it in the news, though. They're selling something else.

Awakening to higher consciousness is what is going to save us. It's happening right now on a grassroots level. And you're a part of it—one of the forerunners.

You are ahead of the bell curve. You are here to help shift the collective consciousness. As you love yourself and others, you change the planet. As you do that little extra bit each day, you'll find inner peace, no matter what's going on around you.

Ask your angels and guides to help you stay focused on our world at peace and in harmony.

Next, we delve into how you affect our collective consciousness.

"Things are not getting worse. They are getting uncovered.
We must hold each other tight and continue to pull back the veil."
—Veronica Entwistle, author

Day 54

For eons, fear has led our collective consciousness. Instead, allow your angels to guide you. Through your example, the collective consciousness will be raised.

You Are Helping Shift the Collective.

The collective consciousness is moving toward a more love-based existence. You are an essential part of that shift. One of the ways you can help is to not play the fear game about money. By doing so, you energetically create a pathway that makes it easier for others to do the same. When you embrace the diversity in people (religion, appearance, belief systems, etc.), you help shift the collective in the direction of acceptance as well.

It is imperative to feel forgiveness, compassion, gratitude and unconditional love. When you are feeling love-based emotions, your vibration rises. The increase enables you to act like a tuning fork, giving those around you an energetic upgrade, raising their vibration into higher love-based frequencies.

Higher vibrations raise your consciousness. In this higher state of consciousness, you awaken. Your thoughts and actions are more oriented toward love, and you have a strong desire to be of service to others.

Higher consciousness is the answer to solving the world's current problems. We cannot use the same lower consciousness that created the chaos in the first place. This need is why the planet is currently undergoing rising consciousness in a mass awakening, individually and collectively.

Angels and Guides Are Assisting in Unprecedented Numbers to Raise Our Collective Consciousness.

Many of you chose to incarnate at this auspicious time to help with this planetary transformation. You incarnated to add specific energies to the collective—the Oneness that embraces us. As you awaken in consciousness, that knowledge is added to the unified field of humans.

Your awakening makes it easier for others to awaken. It has been scientifically proven through the Hundredth Monkey Effect how this phenomenon happens. It's a theory that postulates that once a critical number of members of one group exhibit a new behavior, it spreads from that group to other related groups.

The theory was discovered by scientists studying Snow Monkeys on a Japanese island. They observed a female monkey teach another monkey how to wash the sand off their food in the ocean. The second monkey taught another who taught another and so on. Eventually all the monkeys on the island were washing their food in the ocean.

When the hundredth monkey learned the process, it spread to monkeys worldwide. Soon monkeys everywhere were all washing their food. When a tipping point is achieved, there is a spontaneous shift in consciousness. When a critical mass is reached, the new behavior becomes part of the collective consciousness.

Our collective consciousness is radically affected by a unified field. You are here to add to the tipping point of the unified field affecting the collective consciousness.

We have *never* had this level of assistance from the other side of the veil. They are here to help our world become more peaceful and harmonious by raising our collective consciousness.

In the next lesson, we discuss your specific role in shifting the collective consciousness.

> *"We cannot solve our problems with the same thinking* (consciousness) *we used when we created them."*
> —Albert Einstein

Day 55

Create in Your Life What You Wish to See in the World.

One of the reasons you incarnated at this time is because you have important work to do. You *enthusiastically* volunteered to add to the tipping point that will help raise the collective consciousness. You agreed to bring specific energies to the planet, such as compassion, forgiveness, acceptance, and love. You will not see the full fruition of this higher consciousness, but those being born now will.

It is very important to pay attention to the types of energy your thoughts and emotions create. It is affecting you and everyone around you. Whenever you feel hopeless, anxious or angry, you are energetically adding those harmful, lower-vibrational frequencies to the collective. Whenever you are feeling happy, acceptance or love, you are raising the vibration of the collective.

If you want to make a positive difference in the world, engage in small acts of kindness, compassion and unconditional love. You didn't come here to add more angst, fear or depression.

It would also be extremely helpful to hold a vision in your mind of the world at peace and in harmony. Create peace in your life first. If you feel called to act against what is happening in the world, wonderful. Just react from your heart and not out of fear and anger. If you respond with anger, they will push back.

You Volunteered to Play an Essential Role in Shifting the Collective Consciousness.

If you have already awakened, you likely feel like you no longer fit in with your family, friends or this world. It may seem like we live in an extremely primitive world. You may even feel that you do not want to be here anymore.

You are a few generations ahead of the birth of this higher consciousness. You are a forerunner. Again, you are at the beginning of the bell curve of the higher vibrations raising us into the fifth dimension.

This grassroots movement is happening right now. Some of us will arrive sooner than others into these fifth-dimensional frequencies. Be patient with those who are in the beginning stages of enlightenment. Accept and honor others' choices while they move at their own pace toward higher consciousness.

What you are doing is vital and no small thing. We currently could use more positive thoughts and actions, and engagement with angelic helpers, if you want to volunteer for extra credit.

Next, we expand on how your ego manipulates you.

We are the ones we have been waiting for.

Day 56

Increased Consciousness Awakens You to Your Ego's Agonizing Manipulations.

The more conscious you are, the more you rise above your ego with its illusions, distortions, and pain. When you're living in an unconscious state, the ego manipulates and controls you. The current chaos of the world is a perfect example of what happens when the ego is running the show.

Once you awaken to what your ego is doing, it loses its power over you. Accelerating your awakening is an effective way to break free and find lasting happiness and peace.

As you awaken to your true Divine nature, you stop listening to your ego. You make different choices that are more positive, not driven by fear or greed. You also confront your fears, because you realize that they are deliberately placed in your path to be overcome.

With this shift into higher consciousness, you understand how a simple kind gesture can affect many people. For example, when you open the door for a stranger, it's likely that person will then do the same thing for others. Your small act of kindness becomes multiplied into many kind acts. You create the same positive effect when you smile at someone or let another car merge into traffic ahead of you.

This Lifetime Is About Releasing Your Ego's Painful Grip on You.

As you grow in consciousness, you realize that living in the past or future is a clever distraction created by your ego to keep you from staying in the present. The present is where your power lies, where you create from, and all there is really.

As you slowly transcend the ego, you continue to reach higher levels of awakening and become more enlightened. It's the path every single one of us is on and our ultimate goal. *Everyone* will get there eventually.

You also come to realize that you are a fractal of Divine Source. There's nothing that must be "done" to become the Divine Source because you already *are* the I Am. It's about remembering who you truly are and allowing your Divine Nature to shine through. You are part of the Oneness, not separate from Divine Source or everyone else. We are all one.

Your egoic mind has dirtied the lens with its misperceptions and false identities to obscure your vision. You clean the lens by removing the ego's grimy layers of fear, distortions, and lies. The clarity allows you to see clearly and wake up.

To accelerate the awakening process, *focus on mindfulness throughout your day*. Am I living in the present or has my frustrated mind dragged me back into the past to replay my victim story? When I encounter someone who makes choices different than I'd make, am I reacting with an open, nonjudgmental heart, or with a conditioned mind with expectations of what's "right" and "wrong"?

Rather than being on autopilot, with your ego steering the vehicle, consciously increase awareness as you go about your day. Do not allow your ego to deliberately drive down back alleys that push you into pain and struggle. This lifetime is about stepping off the ego's crazy ride. Or do you need another lifetime or lifetimes to finally stop allowing your ego to unconsciously control you? It's fine if you do.

Next, we explore how to accelerate your awakening.

> *"Do small things with great love."*
> —Mother Teresa

Day 57

The big picture is greater than yourself. Viewing the world from beyond your ego will give you a new perspective, unbiased by false identity, and allow Divine Source to work through you unencumbered.

Release All of Your Identities.

While there are ways to accelerate your spiritual awakening, similarly there are also ways to delay it. Identifying with your ego is one of them. Who do you imagine yourself to be? Do you think of yourself in terms of your gender, profession or age? Maybe you identify with your characteristics or emotions, and consider yourself to be humorous, smart, upbeat or sad. Your answers will help you understand how you see yourself.

Let go of all these identities. All of them. You are *none* of the identities your ego is clinging to so desperately. You're the one having the thoughts, feeling the feelings, playing the different roles. Instead of thinking, *"I'm an average, middle-aged housewife,"* think *"I'm having a thought which is telling me that I'm an average, middle-aged housewife."*

What's left when you release all the labels you've attached to your sense of self and the stories you tell yourself? That's the place you want to get to as often as possible. You simply become a witness to what flows in the moment. Being a witness, or observer, isn't an identity, but rather a state of being.

Live Daily as a Nonpartisan Witness.

When you are a witness, you're experiencing everything beyond the limitations of your ego's beliefs and identities. That's a very different, untainted world. That is where you're able to feel the sense of Oneness. You know you are a part of It and that It is an inseparable part of you.

The best way to accelerate your awakening is when you're faced with any choice, decide whether to approach it through your ego's identities and beliefs or from a witness state. What you'll come to realize is that *Divine Source* is the one observing, feeling, walking, breathing *through* you. It's not any of your ego's false identities.

Observe like an Anthropologist.

Most people have a gradual awakening process that may take years or lifetimes to accomplish. You'll arrive there faster if you get in the habit of being an observer rather than reacting with your ego's baggage.

When sharing a meal with family, coworkers or friends, it might help to imagine you are from a foreign country. It makes it easier to simply sit back and observe rather than get pulled in by the ego's judgments and reactions.

Next, we will discuss what happens when politicians drive you to anger.

"The ego isn't wrong; it's just unconscious. When you observe the ego in yourself, you are beginning to go beyond it... How could humanity have been taken in by this for so long?"
—Eckhart Tolle, spiritual teacher, best-selling author

Day 58

> *In today's world, many will deliberately try to keep you in fear,*
> *overwhelm and confusion. Do not allow yourself to be controlled.*

Everyone Agreed on a Soul Level to Play the Different Roles.

It's hard to view the news these days and not feel disgusted or downright hatred toward certain politicians. The harm they are causing targeted groups and the environment can make even the most passive observers enraged.

When you feel hatred for someone, your daily thoughts become commingled with that toxic negativity. It's easier to get pulled downward and spiral into lower frequencies. When you're in these lower frequencies, you engage more often in lower-vibrational emotions like depression, anger, and despair. It becomes a vicious cycle of unhealthy thoughts and feelings that affect you and those around you.

What's happening globally is designed to help us all grow in consciousness faster. It's also done to get our attention and spur us into action *now!* If things weren't so outrageous, we'd go back to our unconscious living.

What's currently happening politically is *deliberately* shaking us out of our apathy so we will realize what's important and protect it: a healthy planet, equality, and fairness, for example. The most despised politicians are effective catalysts, unknowingly producing this awakening and much needed change.

We're intentionally controlled by being negative, divided and judgmental—anything but unified and compassionate. Those in power know it's easier to manipulate us when we feel fearful, overwhelmed and powerless—that, let's say, North Korea could bomb us at any moment. (FYI, nuclear bombing is *not* going to happen. Benevolent beings will continue to stop all nuclear attacks. They will not allow Earth and the surrounding planets to be destroyed.)

All negative emotions become loosh. The definition of loosh is "energy

124

produced by humans that others use to feed on." Stop creating the loosh that feeds the darkness.

It's also helpful to keep in mind that everyone agreed to play different roles at this Earth school. We are all at once teachers and students.

You're Here to Add Love-Based Emotions to the Planet.

You aren't here to add negativity with your criticism, intolerance, and anger. You *certainly* aren't here to judge the primitiveness and unenlightenment of the Earth's Homo Sapiens.

Take a step back and remember another reason why you're here. You signed up to be a pathmaker. You "stood in line" to be here as we shift, one by one, into an awakened state of higher consciousness and enlightenment.

You may not remember it, but you chose to bring love and higher consciousness to the planet and help with the mass collective transformation. It goes back to the Hundredth Monkey phenomenon. Everyone is connected by a unified field of consciousness.

Leaps in consciousness are achieved when a critical mass point is reached. You're here to add to the tipping point and move us into enlightenment and love. (Psst, the mass tipping point needed isn't that high.) As you engage in an enlightened way of living with compassion and forgiveness, your positive energy adds to the collective tipping point and makes it easier for others to do the same.

Do Not Allow Politicians to Pull You into Lower Frequencies.

Here's your soul's pop quiz at Earth school: Are you going to allow certain politicians to drag you down into lower-vibrational emotions like hatred? The planet and collective certainly don't need more of that, and that's not why you're here. Or are you going to feel compassion and forgiveness?

Your soul's passion is making progress and moving forward in love. Soul evolution requires releasing your mind's negativity and responding more and more with your Divine nature of extraordinary love, compassion, and forgiveness. Overcoming *any* negativity will help you make giant leaps forward.

Tremendous growth opportunities await each and every one of us! The answer is *always* to react from your heart, not your enraged mind. You don't have to like what's occurring but accept that it's designed for our growth. If you can't find acceptance, at least aim for being neutral about certain people. They aren't ready to open up to love and truly be of service to others.

Recognize the most hated politicians are *specifically* here to awaken us into action. If you feel guided, help people register to vote or run for office yourself because it feels like the right thing to do, not out of outrage and fear. Do any number of helpful things, but whatever you do, react from your heart, not your frustrated, angry mind.

The world will change when we change and respond from a higher consciousness with compassion, forgiveness, and love. That's happening one-by-one worldwide right this moment—and you are a part of that. When you approach things with your heart and allow love and forgiveness to flow through you, the world will reflect it. That's what you're here to master. That's your way of being of service.

Next, we dive into how to find peace even when horrific events happen.

"Once you awaken, you will have no interest in judging those who sleep."
—James Blanchard, former diplomat

Day 59

Everyone on a soul level has agreed to go through the ravages of the coronavirus crisis as part of our awakening process.

Being Judgmental Comes from Fear.

We tend to judge others without knowing we do it. It happens all day long. It's another reason to stay in the present rather than operate on autopilot.

From a young age, we're taught what's appropriate. We're each raised with different values and beliefs. We each have our comfort zones. It might be time to move out of the box, step outside your comfort zone. Be more open-minded towards other viewpoints and lifestyles. If you notice a persistent judgment, take a moment to reflect on it. Time to root out your underlying fear or insecurities behind that judgment.

Everyone Is Doing the Best They Can at Their Stage of Soul Development.

Fear is the main culprit behind most judgments. You've determined what is "right" and "wrong," what is acceptable and what is not. When you don't like those who are "different," it is because they are not living by your "rules" and standards.

Often being judgmental is less about them and more about your insecurities and inadequacies. You try to feel better about yourself by putting others down, often for the very thing that makes you insecure. Learn to love and accept yourself *exactly* as you are and cherish the shadow in you as much as you do the light. When you stop judging yourself, you'll stop judging others.

Each one of us is growing at our own pace. It's easier to have compassion when you realize everyone is doing the best they can with where they are in their stage of development.

Everyone Involved in a Horrific Event Agreed on a Soul Level to Participate.

It's easy to judge when we don't know why horrible things happen. The reasons involve shifting the collective consciousness. For instance, years ago, a gunman entered an Amish school and held the children as prisoners. He killed all the schoolchildren and then himself.

Knowing the killer's family were also grieving, the Amish community compassionately invited them to the funeral for the children. The Amish demonstrated extreme compassion and forgiveness.

You cannot judge *anyone* in this catastrophe because you do not know the complete picture. Each of the participants involved agreed on a soul level to undergo this awful tragedy. They understood this would teach the world deeper levels of compassion and forgiveness.

Every disaster occurs with the willingness, on a soul level, of everyone involved, including wildlife. Disasters like the Valdez oil spill required willingness on a soul level of the wildlife harmed and killed. The disastrous spill changed crucial laws regarding the transportation of oil to prevent future spills. The Fukushima disaster stopped the construction of planned nuclear power plants.

Next, we will explore how stillness and mindfulness are essential to a happier, more peaceful life.

> *"Do the best you can until you know better.*
> *Then when you know better, do better."*
> —Maya Angelou

Day 60

The Mind is a Never-Ending Narrator.

Our minds jump from one thought to another. We have a hard time focusing. Few of us live in the moment. Our minds are in a perpetual state of busyness and distraction. The answer is to quiet your mind.

A quiet mind can focus better than a restless one. Finding stillness enables you to control your thoughts and fears. When you are mindful of the present, your mind will naturally calm down.

Mindfulness Brings Clarity, Peace, and Serenity.

There are many ways to cultivate stillness throughout your busy day. One simple method is to create time in your day to sit for just a moment. Obviously, a daily practice of meditation is best, but you can also find brief moments of doing and thinking about nothing. Even in a noisy office or crowded airport, you can stop the mind's chatter and find stillness inside yourself.

No matter how busy your schedule, you can take a minute to be more present. Sit still and assess your state of mind. What are you feeling? Do not judge your feelings: simply observe them. Why are you feeling this way?

Next, focus on your body. Engage all your senses. Feel the air against your skin. What do you see, hear, taste and smell? Take those sensations to an even greater depth. What do you hear in the distance? Be completely immersed in the moment.

You practice mindfulness when you bring your focus to the present. Most anxiety is caused by living in the past or future. The past is your memories and the future is your imagination. Bring yourself back to the present whenever your thoughts are drifting elsewhere. Your power is in the present moment.

It might help to release your thoughts if you write a list. Write down what's going through your mind: the emails, errands, tasks to complete, calls to make. Once your mind is clear, sit in stillness for a few moments. You will find peace and feel replenished.

> *By quieting your mind throughout the day, you will*
> *"hear" the subtle messages from angels and guides.*

Guided Meditations

For an **easy general meditation**, see Day 33.

To **relieve anxiety and fears**, use Serenity Meditation below.

For a meditation to **communicate with your guides and angel**, see Day 20.

If you are having **financial difficulty**, use Meditation for Prosperity below.

If **you've lost a loved one**, use Meditation for Grief below.

To **unwind**, use Relaxation Meditation below.

For a meditation to **help heal the world**, use Meditation for the World below.

If **your loved one has an illness**, use Meditation for a Loved One below.

General Meditation:

1. Seated in a comfortable position, close your eyes and take three deep breaths. Slowly inhale and exhale. Relax a little more with each breath.

2. Place your focus on the slow, steady rhythm of your breathing. Follow your breath as you inhale air into your lungs and slowly exhale out your nose.

3. When thoughts enter your mind, gently bring your attention back to your breathing.

4. (Insert specific meditation here.)

5. When you are ready to end the meditation, imagine your feet growing roots all the way to the center of the Earth. Take three deep, slow breaths and open your eyes.

Serenity Meditation

- Follow Steps 1-3 in the General Meditation.
- For Step 4, use the following:

Scan your body for areas that are tense. Breathe into those areas and release the tension.

Hand over all your concerns to your angels and guides. Ask them to help you resolve those issues and find peace of mind.

Think of some way to help someone this week.

Feel gratitude for 6-10 people or things in your life.

- Follow Step 5 to conclude the meditation.

Meditation for Prosperity

- Follow Steps 1-3 in the General Meditation.
- For Step 4, use the following:

Tell your guardian angel where you are having financial difficulties. Ask them to bring you prosperity to help with those finances.

Ask your angel to help ensure you are taken care of and develop trust in their ability to help you.

- Follow Step 5 to conclude the meditation.

Meditation for Grief

- Follow Steps 1-3 in the General Meditation.
- For Step 4, use the following:

Feel your chest rise and fall with each breath. Feel grief well up within you. Imagine this pain now cascading over you like an ocean wave and flowing down and out your body.

Next, imagine your deceased loved one at peace with a smile on their face. Tell them whatever you want to say. Converse with them in your mind for as long as you need. Hand all your sorrow to them. They are happy and relieved to take this burden from you. When you are ready, say your goodbyes for the moment.

- Follow Step 5 to conclude the meditation.

Relaxation Meditation

- Follow Steps 1-3 in the General Meditation.
- For Step 4, use the following:

Imagine a peaceful setting. Add details using all five senses.

Shift your focus to your solar plexus. Inhale the energy of peace, exhale any tension. Continue inhaling and exhaling whatever you want until you feel relaxed.

- Follow Step 5 to conclude the meditation.

Meditation for the World

- Follow Steps 1-3 in the General Meditation.
- For Step 4, use the following:

In your mind, imagine a world at peace and harmony. What does that look like in your daily life?

Next, envision legions of angels encircling the globe. Imagine they are sending waves of love engulfing the entire planet. Send these immensely devoted angels your gratitude and love.

- Follow Step 5 to conclude the meditation.

Meditation for a Loved One

- Follow Steps 1-3 in the General Meditation.

- For Step 4, use the following:

Call forward a golden white healing light. Engage this healing light to flow into your loved one. Do this for 3-5 minutes.

- Follow Step 5 to conclude the meditation.

About the Author

ROBBIE HOLZ

Robbie's life was drastically altered in 1985. After a difficult thirty-six-hour delivery, while giving birth to her only child, Robbie was given a blood transfusion to "perk her up faster." Unfortunately, the transfusion was tainted with Hepatitis C.

When Western medicine was no longer able to help her, Robbie set out to find alternative ways to survive and recover. She ultimately healed herself of Hepatitis C, fibromyalgia, chronic fatigue syndrome and treatment-induced temporary brain damage, described in her award-winning memoir, *Aboriginal Secrets of Awakening.*

While on her quest for wellness, Robbie met Dr. Gary Holz, an award-winning physicist, PsychoNeuroImmunologist and alternative healer. The two eventually married. Gary taught her the aboriginal healing techniques he learned from his encounter with remote Outback Australian aboriginal tribespeople, chronicled in his best-selling memoir, *Secrets of Aboriginal Healing.*

Like her husband, Robbie has had first-hand experiences with aboriginal tribespeople in the Australian Outback. She joined Gary in teaching the over 60,000-year-old aboriginal healing system, revealed at the tribe's request.

Started in 1995, their healing practice centered on aboriginal healing principles, quantum physics and PsychoNeuroImmunology—using the mind to heal the body.

Robbie is an internationally respected healer, medium and speaker, and remains dedicated to helping people worldwide. Her website is www. holzwellness.com.

Made in the USA
Monee, IL
13 November 2024